SOLVING THE BRAND PUZZLE®

How to define and develop a complete brand.

SOLVING THE BRAND PUZZLE®

How to define and develop a complete brand.

ROBERT MICHAUD

HUDSON
HOUSE

FIRST EDITION
ISBN 978-1-58776-930-6
Library of Congress catalog card number: 2012951225

Manufactured in the United States of America
NetPublications, Inc
675 Dutchess Turnpike, Poughkeepsie, NY 12603
www.hudsonhousepub.com (800) 724-1100

675 Dutchess Turnpike, Poughkeepsie, NY 12603
www.hudsonhousepub.com (800) 724-1100

Table of Contents

Acknowledgements

Solving the Brand Puzzle took a little over two years to complete. It never would have happened without the collaborative support of my wife, KC Grapes. KC's attention to readability is why the book makes any sense at all. I humbly admit I could not have done it without her. Her insistence that every word must further the story turned my concept into something worth sharing with readers. You might say KC helped me solve the writing puzzle.

My expanded editing community included my daughter, Kestrel Michaud, who is great at crossing the "Ts", and her husband, Alex Taylor, who provided a valuable left-brain perspective. Kestrel and Alex are products of the digital age and were quick to mention, early on in the project, that the book did not adequately address websites and technology. Chapter 6, The Digital Brand, was the result of their input.

Jennifer Farley was our final editor. She is a journalist and came aboard to help with citations and other technical matters. In the process, she got "sucked in" and provided some great content for the story.

Lizbeth Nauta put the finishing touches on the style formatting. She also prepared the manuscript for publication. If KC and Jennifer helped *Solving the Brand Puzzle* read like a book, Lizbeth helped make it look and feel like a book.

As you might expect, a 40-year career in customer service, marketing, and advertising connected me with many people from whom I have learned much. At the top of that list I would have to place Chuck Urtin, about whom you will read in the book.

Chuck was the person who helped me realize that there isn't a rivalry between left brain and right brain thinkers, only a gap in understanding. Once I came to that realization, I never thought of creative and technical thinkers in the same way ever again. I realized that when the two sides collaborate, great things happen. I would forever strive to transform creative ideas into processes that left brain thinkers could understand. I am indebted to Chuck for this epiphany.

Lastly, to the many friends and colleagues who cheered the project on and patiently waited for the result, I'm indebted to you for your support.

An Introduction to Customer Service

Thrown Out of an Irish Pub

One of the strangest examples of customer service I've ever experienced was on the night I was thrown out of an Irish pub. I had been touring Savannah, Georgia, on July 31, 2007, with my two teenage daughters and their friend. After a long day exploring the historic district, we were in great spirits and ready to wind down at one of the local restaurants.

We chose an Irish pub for dinner and walked in just before six o'clock. To our delight, a musician came into the dining room at six and started playing Irish tunes. Since I like Irish music, I began singing along with him to "Whiskey in the Jar," "Fiddler's Green," and "Black and Tans."

While enjoying our dinner, we heard thunder outside and realized it had started to rain…hard. I took notice of the Weather Channel, which was playing on a silenced, big-screen TV hanging in the upper corner of the dining room. Apparently, all hell was breaking loose out there. The TV screen was declaring "Breaking News" in Savannah, Georgia. An Armageddon-like line of storms was bearing down on us. The anchor was advising local residents to seek shelter.

Looking out the restaurant window, the other side of the street was not visible through the sideways-blowing wall of rain. Although by now we had finished our meal, the violent weather had not abated. For the safety of my kids, I decided to ride this storm out right where we were.

It was at this moment that the manager came up to our table to inform me that we had to leave. My response was, "You have got to be joking!"

I looked up at the TV to see more "Breaking News" from Savannah. Someone had been struck by lightning and died.[1] The manager was squatting down on my left, trying to be discreet about throwing me and my family out of his pub. At the same time, the TV was warning people in Savannah to stay inside! Every kind of warning imaginable was plastered on the screen: tornado warnings, severe thunderstorm warnings, wind, hail, and flash floods. The only thing missing was a hurricane warning!

"Why are you doing this?" I asked.

He mumbled something about the law in Savannah prohibiting minors in a bar after seven o'clock. It was now 7:30. I couldn't believe what I was hearing. I pointed out that we had not been informed of this when we chose his restaurant for dinner. He was not swayed.

"I know you are upset," he insisted, "but you have to go."

My next question, "Why didn't you let us know before we sat down to dinner?" met with no explanation.

He continued to state, "The police strictly enforce the ordinance."

I countered "OK, then call the cops. Let's see if they want to risk the safety of my family out there or cut us a break for an hour until the storm of the decade passes."

A quick glance to the TV on the right revealed a fresh round of "Breaking News." The Savannah storm was making national news headlines, and my family and I were being thrown out of an Irish pub into the teeth of it.

The manager then offered a compromise, which I had some trouble hearing above a rather well done rendition of "Irish Rover," with impromptu percussion provided by claps of thunder.

The manager said, "If you and your kids wait outside under the awning, I'll go get my car. Then I'll drive you to your car so you can come back and get the rest of your group. But everyone has to wait outside. They cannot wait in here."

"Why not just call the cops?" I asked again. "In fact, I'll call them. I'd like to hear what they have to say," as I reached for my cell phone.

"No, please," he begged, "the owner will be very upset if the police come."

"Alright, fine." I finally gave up and accepted his offer. I paid the bill, with no tip, and we got up to leave. The Irish singer, thinking he had a captive fan for at least the duration of the storm, was surprised and disappointed.

When he asked what was going on I answered, "Sorry, we've been told to leave."

His jaw dropped in disbelief.

The deal played out as promised. We huddled under the awning outside, and waited for the manager to build up his nerve to run out into the storm. When he finally decided to go, he was drenched within seconds. It was as though someone was on the second floor waiting to ambush him with a bucket of water. After about ten minutes (his car must have been several blocks away) he pulled up to the curb. Leaving my three teenagers under the awning, I ran for his car door. As promised, he drove me to my car, then still had to go park his car and run back through the torrential downpour to his post at the pub. I returned to the pub and picked up my family, amazed at the total absence of common sense that surrounded the whole incident.

Thinking about this remarkable experience prompts the question, "What would you have done in this situation?" Here was a manager who rigidly enforced a law that was intended to safeguard children. Yet, in so doing, he risked the safety of my three children. What should he have done instead? The answer is simple: Bend the rule for an hour or so until the storm passed.

As you will learn in *Solving the Brand Puzzle*, safety is an important brand attribute. In fact, it usually trumps EVERYTHING.

What is a brand? How is a complete brand different?

The word "brand" is confusing because it is used in many ways. It generally refers to a unique symbol, such as a logo or name, which is used to distinguish a company or product from others in the market.

In the Wild West, ranchers used to burn a distinguishing symbol on the rumps of their cattle to identify them on the open range. The cattlemen called this symbol their brand. Today, examples of distinguishing symbols include the Coca-Cola and Harley Davidson logos, Target's red bull's eye, and Nike's "swoosh." These are great examples, but they refer only to the traditional definition of brand which focuses on the visual elements alone.

A complete brand, on the other hand, is comprised of a lot more than just visual identity. It takes into account other sensory input: In a restaurant, the taste of the food, the sound of the background music, the aroma of the coffee, and the feel of the upholstery all make an impression. Other non-sensory attributes, such as safety, efficiency, and customer service also influence perception. These all play a role in defining a complete brand and how a brand is perceived by the customer. *Solving the Brand Puzzle* probes all the "nitty-gritty" details of what makes a brand complete.

When a company strives to build a brand that includes company-wide commitments and customer promises, it takes a lot more than a logo to achieve success. A strategic, grand scale program is required to ensure that the brand is embodied in the very culture of the company. Every employee must live and breathe it. *Solving the Brand Puzzle* goes far beyond creating a visual identity and will demonstrate how you can build a brand that is complete.

The Walt Disney Company offers a great example of a complete brand. It delivers a consistent customer experience whether at one of its hotels, theme parks, restaurants, cruise ships, or even on a parking shuttle tram. Although Disney's Mickey Mouse logo is among the most recognized in the world, it's not the logo that delivers the world-class Disney customer experience. Disney's successful deployment of a complete brand has given the company this distinction.

How does Disney get all of its 50,000+ employees to deliver

consistent service excellence? The answer is this: Disney pioneered a method of executing the goals of the company's strategic vision from its leadership team down to every employee in every division of the organization. In doing so, it established a culture that assures a consistent sensory experience for every guest. Why is this important? The answer is because Disney has mastered a way to take control of how its brand is perceived by its customers.

Perception is important. Your company's brand isn't what you think it is, but rather what your customer perceives it to be. Many companies think they know how they are perceived by the public. They may feel they have control over their customers' perceptions, but they could be entirely wrong. Have you ever eaten at a restaurant where the food was good, yet your lasting impression was of a dirty restroom or a crabby server? The owner likely believed he was delivering a good customer experience based on the quality of his food. What he did not realize was that your opinion of the restaurant was formed by your total experience, which went beyond the quality of the food. His perception was not in alignment with your perception of his business. Until the owner develops his complete brand, he will not be in control of how his company is perceived.

Why does having a complete brand matter?

Without a complete brand, a company cannot ensure it will thrive and sustain its success far into the future. Today, customer experience is being held to a higher standard. Before the proliferation of national chain stores in the suburbs, service quality was determined by the personalities of the employees of the small businesses on Main Street. Some of the shop owners were "nice," others "rude;" some shops "quaint," others "messy." Things have certainly changed. Customer service is now an integral part of the strategic goals of many of America's largest and most successful organizations. This expansion and elevation of customer service standards has raised the expectations of the consumer. Now, there are endless choices and numerous competitors vying for that consumer's patronage. Customers have become less tolerant of a bad customer experience today than they had been in the past. Before there was an internet, unsatisfied customers would tell their friends about a bad experience face-to-face. Today they can jump on Facebook, Twitter, Angie's List, chat channels, and numerous other social media venues to tell the world!

Consider what this means to "mom-and-pop" businesses across America who don't have access to world-class strategic planning, management development, staff training, and visual design. Let's contemplate, for example, a local Italian bistro owner's challenge. His Mediterranean-themed dining venue used to compete only with other local restaurants. Food quality, service, and atmosphere were a reflection of the owners' skill, personality, and hard work. Today, that same bistro competes with numerous national chains. These include Olive Garden, the popular family-friendly Italian restaurant subsidiary of Darden, which operates nearly 1,900 themed restaurants across America.

Olive Garden's menu items are professionally designed and tested. Consistent food quality is assured because Darden operates its own food distribution company. Through training and brand development, service and food quality are consistent across the entire chain. Atmosphere and identity are also consistent and designed to enhance the dining experience. This is why there is almost always a wait for a table at Olive Garden. Guests go to Olive Garden for good food and go back because they enjoy the experience.

The local Italian bistro's challenge is the same as that faced by the local hardware store competing with Lowe's, the local drug store competing with Walgreens, and the main street, USA specialty retailer competing with Walmart. The standards have been elevated to a new level of sophistication by large companies. In today's competitive world, every company needs to solve its brand puzzle in order to stay "in the game." This book will help you solve your brand puzzle.

Speaking of "the game," objective number one is making money. A complete brand directly affects profitability.

Ask the Walt Disney Company. This organization's strategic focus on customer experience increases profit. By driving profit, they can continue to invest in their restaurants, attractions, and resorts. In Disney's world, this is an investment in the experience they deliver. Does it work for them? Incredibly well! On February 26, 1971, one share of Disney stock traded for $177.75. The stock split on five occasions during the next four decades and transformed that single share into 192 shares. On December 14, 2012, Disney stock was trading at $48.67[2]. When you do the math, 192 shares multiplied by $48.67 turns that single share of $177.75, in 1971, into a value of $9,344.64 today. Any questions?

Solving the Brand Puzzle is for everyone

The *Solving the Brand Puzzle* approach applies to theme parks, national restaurant chains, big-box retailers, mom-and-pop businesses, and even railroads, just to name a few. We have already touched on theme parks and restaurant chains ... but railroads? In *Solving the Brand Puzzle* we'll take a ride on a commuter rail "terror train" and look at how a railroad can deliver a bad customer experience. Who would think a railroad would need to be concerned about a complete brand? As stated earlier, *Solving the Brand Puzzle* is for everyone.

Today, the internet has created a new challenge in providing a memorable customer experience. Much of e-commerce takes place in an environment with little direct human interaction. To counter that impersonal feeling, Amazon.com and other online retailers "personalize" the automated process. We think it's "cool" when Amazon makes an intuitive book or music suggestion as soon as we add something to our shopping carts. In contrast, when ordering by phone, or making a store purchase, we find it annoying when an employee pushes us to purchase additional products and services. Interesting, isn't it? *Solving the Brand Puzzle* will take a closer look at the online customer experience in chapter six.

Solving the Brand Puzzle is even beneficial to individuals. Consider a waitress. She may not think of herself as having a "personal brand," but her behavior, appearance, and attitude are indeed the attributes that determine how others perceive her. It seems logical to assume that a waitress who is professional, polite, courteous, has a warm smile, anticipates customers' needs, gets the orders right, and delivers prompt service, would earn larger tips than one who is not.

I learned my first "good service pays" lesson when I was eight years old. I used to help my mom at Janvier's Food Store, the neighborhood grocery store she operated. Her store was in a tenement district in New Bedford, Massachusetts. The customers were hard working, blue collar, textile mill workers. In an era before there were supermarkets, one of my mom's differentiators was that her store delivered grocery orders. Customers called her store and gave their orders over the phone. Later that day, one of her employees would go deliver the orders, similar to what a pizzeria does today.

I used to tag along on the delivery route. Mom's drivers soon realized they could send "the kid" up three flights of stairs with the grocery orders while they slacked off in the car. I never complained because while they were slacking, I was getting the tips! People would marvel at the hard working, polite, smiling kid and tip 50 cents or a dollar on a regular basis. For an eight year old back in the sixties, this was big money!

The simple lesson I learned back then, about how providing great service makes money, is just as important today. Attentive and considerate service solidifies customer relationships and ultimately drives profit.

The puzzle pieces that make up a complete brand

A complete brand results from the integration of four essential pieces. They are:
- Strategic Vision
- Management
- Culture
- Sensory Experience

In this book, we will evaluate companies based on these four components. Every company has its own personality made up of characteristics that set it apart from all others. Just as every person has a personality unique to him or her, so do companies. Some companies choose to focus on price, others on innovation, and still others on customer experience. Regardless of the strategic emphasis, for a company to realize its full potential it must integrate all four pieces of the brand puzzle.

Solving the Brand Puzzle will examine such well known brands as Walmart, Disney, Xerox, Darden Restaurants, and others. We will also look at a few you may not know, such as Montano's Shoe Store and GreenPartStore.com, to help you better understand how to develop a complete brand for your business.

Solving the Brand Puzzle will also make you an informed critic by helping you understand why your emotions are triggered, good or bad, as a consumer. Never again will you eat at a restaurant, go shopping, or visit any establishment without having a clear understanding of your customer experience.

An important goal of this book is to break down the abstract concept of brand development into a series of steps that will clarify the process for more technical, left-brain intellects. It will introduce you to a combination of innovative concepts and proven techniques that come together as a comprehensive brand discovery process. This will be useful in bridging the gap between the logical left-brain thinkers and the creative right-brain thinkers of your company. Uniting these thought-leadership resources will be necessary to solve your brand puzzle.

Solving the Brand Puzzle also takes a look at how you can use your company's past experiences, new discoveries, and industry-recognized best practices to build a complete brand. Not only will you learn how to discover your brand, you will learn how to communicate it to your customer, train your staff to deliver it, and build the department-level infrastructure to support it.

One last comment: *Solving the Brand Puzzle* looks at several companies under a "brand" microscope. These brand critiques are not my personal opinions, but they are my perceptions. Having an opinion is fine, but the important question to me is, "What formed my opinion?" The answer is that my perception was formed as a result of how my senses acquired information about the surrounding environment or situation. Understanding what forms perceptions will help you build a better brand. The single most important concept of the book for you to remember is this: A brand is not what a company says it is, but rather how it is perceived by the customer.

CHAPTER 1

The Power of Process
Keeping It Simple

Chuck Urtin, a community banker in Western Pennsylvania, would often say to his staff "keep it simple." For Chuck, problem-solving began with a common sense approach. When a customer had a complaint, if there was any question about how to deal with the problem, Chuck would empathize with the customer. He'd ask his managers, "If you were in the customer's shoes, what would you expect?" In contrast to all the theories and guru-philosophies on the subject of customer service and decision-making, Chuck offered a simple, grass roots, human-values approach to problem solving. In Chuck's world, trusting a "gut feeling" was just as important as "managing by the book."

Chuck grew up in the small factory town of Jeannette, Pennsylvania. His home town, blue-collar work ethic carried him through night school to earn a Masters degree. Eventually, his career led him to becoming the President and CEO of Irwin Bank and Trust Company, a community bank headquartered in Irwin, Pennsylvania, just down the road from his hometown of Jeannette. In spite of Chuck's personal success, he never lost his straightforward, common-sense values.

In 2001, I became Irwin Bank's marketing director. Chuck had hired me away from my own advertising agency to establish a new marketing department at the bank. During the early 2000's, our management team often debated the risky lending practices of our competitors. We could not figure out why some of our competitors increasingly engaged in reckless lending. Despite mounting pressure to loosen our own lending practices, Chuck's simple, common-sense values proved to be prescient, as they ultimately kept Irwin Bank safe and strong. Chuck was not going to allow his bank to get sucked into making bad loans. When it came to considering whether Irwin Bank should get into the game, Chuck's simple rationale led him to say, "If a customer can't afford the loan, we're not going to make the loan." Chuck understood that such risky lending practices were luring consumers to take on more debt than they could realistically afford. Consequently, Irwin Bank's loan portfolio stayed strong, the stock price stayed high, and the bank's foundation remained solid. When the house of cards collapsed on the lending industry, in the great recession of 2008, Chuck would have been justified in saying, "I told you so!"

Chuck and I enjoyed a great relationship. In the five years I spent working for him, I learned that some of life's lessons come from the most unusual people and experiences. Chuck was a typical banker, a classic numbers guy with strong operations skills. In banking, it's all about counting the money. It is a world that revolves around computer systems, workflow procedures, regulations, and the balance sheet. The Maalox bottle is in every bank president's top drawer. They worry about interest rates, the investment portfolio, risk management, technology, loan quality, and all the other left-brain stuff that makes the bank "tick." It is a black and white, step-by-step world to them.

This was Chuck's world, too, until he hired me as his marketing director. Suddenly, Chuck had a right-brain lunatic reporting to him. Not long after I started at the bank, I attended the American Bankers Association School of Bank Marketing and Management. Not only did I learn how Chuck's side of the business worked, but also how my side related to it. It was there that I had an epiphany when one of the instructors declared, "The traditional bank marketing model can no longer be sustained." He reasoned that banks traditionally generate over 90% of their income from the interest earned from loans. But because of the economy, trends in financial services, technology, and regulations, banks would need to change how they do business. More income would have to come from other sources, such as service charges and new products. The traditional business model would have to change. I was enlightened by the instructor's postulation, and inspired by the potential that change could bring to Irwin Bank.

When I returned from the school, I challenged Chuck with questions about new possibilities for the bank. How could we transform our image? How could we revolutionize retail delivery and customer service? How could we create more alternative income streams? How could we improve the sales performance of our staff? The answers were as much an opportunity as they were a challenge, and my vision was to capture these opportunities and package them in a whole new brand for the bank.

Although this was new, right-brain thinking for Chuck, the funny part was he liked it. We spent a lot of time in his office, and sometimes in the board room with our feet on the table, white-boarding the bank's future. He would get very excited when I expounded on a long-range vision for the corporate brand. But our initial discussions often ended with Chuck expressing frustration and commenting, "I love these ideas, but I wish I could understand how to put it all together."

This is where I learned an important lesson: Although my ideas and vision were exciting to Chuck, he could not fully appreciate them, or support them, unless I could present them on his terms in an operational context. Chuck was a left-brain thinker struggling to understand right-brain concepts. His operational viewpoint needed my creative ideas transformed into block diagrams and flow charts.

As luck would have it, I actually already had a good understanding of how to use block diagrams and flow charts in my professional toolbox. Early in my career, I had worked as a Tech Rep at Xerox Corporation, the market leader in office copying machines at the time. The company had developed step-by-step flow charts as trouble-shooting guides for copier repair. These charts walked Tech Reps through a series of questions which, depending upon the answers, would guide them to the next steps. A few simple queries usually managed to isolate a problem, and then a repair procedure could be readily determined. If Xerox could design such a simplified process to teach a right-brainer like me how to survive in the left-brain world of a repair technician, why couldn't I use the same technique to explain the creative process of branding to Chuck?

In his book *A Whole New Mind*[1], best-selling author Dan Pink discusses at length the left-brain, right-brain dilemma. He makes the argument that today's society and economies are transitioning out of the information age and into the conceptual age. Designers, innovators, and "big-picture" thinkers are now becoming equally as important as engineers, "number-crunchers," and computer programmers. Out of necessity, they are all learning to better understand the inter-connected roles they play. A company's success is no longer defined by left-brain thinking, but by how well both left- and right-brain thinkers collaborate. Apple offers a great example. Under the leadership of Steve Jobs, the company used right-brain industrial design, in collaboration with left-brain engineering, to re-invent several different products and businesses, including the cell phone, personal entertainment, animated movie production, and publishing.

Marketers have stereotypically labeled engineers as being pedantic. Conversely, engineers typically dismissed marketers as being out there in the twilight zone. So when marketers have been hired by engineers to promote products, the relationship has often proved fractious. Thinking about Dan Pink's right-brain, left-brain premise, if the engineers had instead collaborated with marketers on writing the owner's manual, maybe more of us would be able to set the clock on the DVD player! And, if such collaboration had not occurred at Apple, perhaps the iPad and iPhone would not exist today. To succeed in today's competitive environment, the gap between engineers and the communicators must be bridged.

I "got it." In my 21 years of experience as a marketing executive and advertising agency owner, I had been waiting for the engineers and business managers to embrace creative development. Now I was beginning to understand the potential in reversing the roles. I wanted to apply their left-brain language of process and structure as a way to communicate abstract, right-brain concepts so they could better understand them.

Eager to bridge the gap between process and creativity in brand development at Irwin Bank, I needed to find a way to transpose my vision into a structured format. I now wanted to take on the challenge of interpreting the abstract concept of branding into a process that Chuck could understand on his terms. Since he wanted it, I was determined to provide it. But I was still a long way from putting the process together and presenting it to Chuck.

Coincidentally, it was around this time I learned a piece of Irwin Bank's history that would ultimately become a critical element of the *Solving the Brand Puzzle* process. The story revolved around one of Irwin Bank's founders, Tobias Berkowitz. In the early 20th century, Tobias owned a clothing store on Main Street in Irwin, Pennsylvania. Besides selling clothing, he also helped scores of European immigrants find a better life in the United States. He arranged their immigration details and provided other needed support upon their arrival in America.

In 1922, Tobias and a handful of other investors pooled $100,000 in capital and founded the Irwin Savings and Trust Company. He saw this as an opportunity to provide financial security for those he had helped and who trusted him with everything in the name of fulfilling their dreams.

The bank grew and quickly prospered until the stock market crash of 1929. On the first day of business following the crash, a crowd of customers formed in front of the bank. They had come to withdraw their savings. Across the street, another financial institution had posted armed guards to prevent a run on that bank. It was a tense environment.

Tobias Berkowitz stepped out of Irwin Savings to address the crowd. He declared, "This bank will not fail! You trusted me with your money before there was a bank and you can trust me now. My promise to you is this: The owners of this bank will invest as much capital as necessary to protect your savings."[2]

The bank's depositors did not withdraw their savings that day and the company went on to prosper. With this statement, made during the most dire of circumstances, Tobias Berkowitz established

Irwin Bank's brand. It was a brand of commitment to taking care of the customer.

I related this forgotten piece of history to Irwin Bank's 40 managers at a quarterly meeting. Everyone in the room was deeply moved by the company's heritage of helping people. However, upon hearing the story, several of the managers questioned why this story had never been communicated to them before. They had a valid point. Why had it not?

Somewhere along the way, as Irwin Bank grew, it lost its connection to Tobias' values. Sure, it had successfully developed processes

Tobias Berkowitz and wife.

to deal with technological advancement and was also managing to keep pace with larger, more sophisticated competitors. However, what had not developed was a process to maintain its historic culture of customer caring. For all of its operational success, the company no longer had a branded culture. Over the years, Irwin Bank's hard-working, dedicated staff had managed operational growth effectively. Now they needed a long range strategic vision to re-establish a company-wide culture which included the forgotten core values of customer caring. This would require a grand-scale commitment that would not just happen by itself. It would need to be designed. My proposal to Chuck would have to include a clearly structured, step-by-step process.

At this point, I understood what needed to be accomplished, but realized we would need outside, expert help. It soon became obvious to me that while there were a lot of experts on branding, most espoused fairly limited theories which focused on just one piece of what I was beginning to recognize as a more complex puzzle. I discovered visual design experts, strategy gurus, management maestros, and finally corporate culture architects. But, my assessment of the Irwin Bank challenge was that it would require a blend of all four areas of expertise. In my research, I had not seen anything resembling the comprehensive approach I was seeking.

It became clear we would need a unique approach that I would have to innovate. Four essential pieces must inter-connect in order to make a brand complete.

The essential pieces needed to solve the Brand Puzzle®

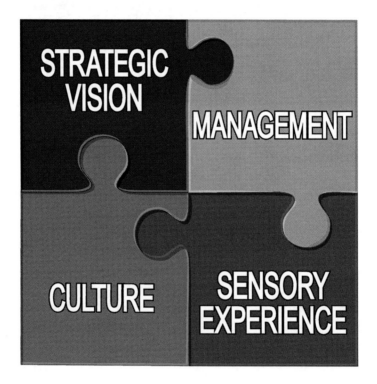

It almost seemed too elementary. But then again, that was the point: Keep it simple. The four pieces, Strategic Vision, Management, Culture, and Sensory Experience, when inter-related, provide a structure for what had been an abstract concept. However, one last step was necessary: Breaking down each category according to appropriate and essential functions, processes, and objectives.

This is how the finished concept eventually looked:

Brand Discovery (Core Values)
    Heritage and Traditions
    Purpose of Business
Brand Cornerstones
    Company Brand Standards
    Staff Behavioral Guidelines
    Customer Brand Statement
    Department Brand Integration
TWSO
    Threats
    Weaknesses
    Strengths
    Opportunities
Strategic Vision
    Statement of Vision
    Strategic Goals

Leadership
    Tactical Plan
    Goals
    Scorecard
    Staff

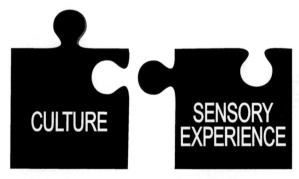

Elements of Culture
    Philosophy
    Products
    Services
    Behaviors
    Actions
    Skills
Consistency
Assessment
Measurement

Brand Manual
    Logo Standards
    Brand Definitions
    Graphics Standards
    Sign Standards
Communications
    Advertising
    Public Relations
    Internal Communications
Total Sensory Appeal

When Chuck first saw how I applied logic to the abstract concept of brand, he "got it." He was now able to understand how the pieces fit together and what would be required to solve Irwin Bank's brand puzzle. At this early stage, it was determined that the management team was strong and would manage the brand establishment process effectively. However, outside expertise would be needed as well.

Irwin Bank went on to spend the next year discovering its brand. It applied several "best of the best" concepts that would ultimately become part of *Solving the Brand Puzzle*. With the help of Jack Salvetti from S.R. Snodgrass Company, a strategic plan was hammered out with a strong emphasis on customer service. With the help of Disney Institute[3], a service culture was designed. And with the help of Kevin Tracey, a principal of the advertising agency Tracey, Edwards, O'Neil, Irwin Bank's brand identity was discovered.

Irwin Bank was on a quest to solve its Brand Puzzle®. For me, the simple, four part model, and lessons learned from Irwin Bank's final process, would become the genesis of *Solving the Brand Puzzle*.

CHAPTER 2

Strategic Vision
Four Hours in Carol Burnett's Bedroom

During the seventies, I was a Beverly Hills cable guy working for Theta Cable Television. I serviced some of Hollywood's most upscale neighborhoods: Beverly Hills, Bel-Air, and Santa Monica. My job was to remedy chronic service problems and requests from high profile subscribers who were placed on what was called the "brushfire" list. Each morning I would pick up the brushfire list and hit the road in cable truck Unit 64.

Although providing customer service to Hollywood's elite could be demanding, it was also exciting and rewarding. I had the great pleasure of meeting some of Hollywood's most famous celebrities at the time, including Kirk Douglas, Natalie Wood, and Cary Grant.

Often, I didn't know whose home I was about to visit because some accounts were listed in the name of a spouse or housekeeper in order to protect privacy. One day, I had a call at the "Hamilton" residence on Doheny Road, just off Sunset Boulevard. I soon realized "Hamilton" was the married name of Carol Burnett, the queen of Hollywood comedy who was at that time enjoying great success with the *Carol Burnett Show*, executive-produced by her husband, Joe Hamilton.

Cable television service had recently been installed in the Hamilton residence. As a new technology, cable was rapidly gaining popularity because it offered better reception and more channels. In those days, although remote control was available with some televisions, it was not available with cable. Instead, a ten-foot wire connected the TV to a cable channel selector box which was about the size of a hardcover novel. This was not a popular feature; not just because of the wires and the unsightly box, but mostly because it prevented use of the remote control buttons that came with the TV.

The remote control problem is what initiated the Hamilton - Burnett household "brushfire" complaint. Joe and Carol were very perturbed that their brand-new, remote-control TV could not be used as desired because of our cable box. The TV was in their bedroom, and to compound the challenge, Joe and Carol wanted independent channel controls from each side of the bed. My task was to figure out how to get two channel selector boxes working with one TV, eliminate the two wires that stretched across the bed, and finally, make the channel selectors function independently. This was going to be a tough job!

I figured out a clever solution for eliminating the unsightly wires. Rather than install the cable boxes at the TV, I put them under the bed. This involved hiding the wires in the walls, a closet, and the attic. That part of the job worked great. However, getting two channel selectors to operate independently, the way the Hamiltons wanted, was a different story. This had never been done before at Theta Cable. I was stumped. After a phone call to one of our engineers, we realized that all I had to do was snip two wires inside the channel selectors. Sure enough, this enabled independent control. The whole job took about four hours.

When Joe and Carol came to see the finished result, I showed them how I managed to hide the cable apparatus and demonstrated how the channel selectors worked. I also proudly informed them that they were the only customers in all of Beverly Hills with such a custom installation!

Joe was extremely pleased. In fact, he was so appreciative of my extra effort and ingenuity that he promptly peeled off $50 in cash for a tip. That was a lot of money back in the mid-seventies, an amount worth over $300 today!

Here is the point: Just like the little boy back at Janvier's Food Store, I had once again used my personality, hard work, and a strong desire to please as a means to earn a generous tip. Over time, I had discovered my own personal brand, and now realized how it was helping me make more money.

This is a simple example of how discovering a brand and putting it to work benefits an individual. However, it is not unlike the brand discovery process every company should strive to achieve.

How Brand Discovery impacts Strategic Vision

It is important for a company to discover the essential elements of its brand in order to use them as an influence in developing a Strategic Vision. Heritage, traditions, and the purpose of a company's business are the elements that make each company unique. These characteristics, which played an important role for the company in the past and continue to influence the present, should play a role in how the company looks toward its future.

Brand Discovery (Core Values)
  Heritage and Traditions
  Purpose of Business
Brand Cornerstones
  Company Brand Standards
  Staff Behavioral Guidelines
  Customer Brand Statement
  Department Brand Integration
TWSO
  Threats
  Weaknesses
  Strengths
  Opportunities
Strategic Vision
  Statement of Vision
  Strategic Goals

Before we discuss the process by which a company develops its Strategic Vision, let's look at why Strategic Visions are important.

Each Strategic Vision is unique

There are many types of Strategic Visions. For example, the hospitality industry's Strategic Vision is built on service quality. Ritz Carlton sets the bar when it comes to service quality in a hotel. Founder Cesar Ritz's philosophy of service and innovation has redefined the luxury hotel experience since the early 1900s.

Other Strategic Visions are based on luxury and affluence, such as those of Seattle-based retailer Nordstrom, Inc. and car maker Lexus, the premium-vehicle division of Japan's Toyota Motor Company. Nordstrom and Lexus are the subjects of countless MBA case studies as "best practice" examples. Still other Strategic Visions focus on being a price leader. One is not necessarily better than the other. The point is that you must have a clear understanding of yours and a good rationale for choosing it.

When it comes to a price-driven Strategic Vision, my favorite example is Wal-Mart Stores, Inc., the world's largest retailer, which serves over 200 million customers a week in 28 countries. I have yet to see a company evoke more emotion in a group discussion than Walmart. I call it "the company people love to hate." However, every Strategic Vision should start with a basic goal to make money. So before we begin analyzing Walmart, let's understand that Walmart knows how to make money. It consistently showed strong income throughout the great recession of 2008.[1] Statistics on Walmart are colossal, especially when it comes to financial returns. For its fiscal year ending in January 2008, Walmart reported $375,000,000,000 in sales. That breaks down to $42,000,000 in sales per hour. When Walmart's reported 5.8% profit margin is factored in, the company generated a cool profit of $35,000... *every minute of every day!*

Not only did fiscal 08's returns represent an 8.6 percent increase over the previous year, the amount of money Walmart earned set a record for any retailer, according to the Bentonville, Arkansas-based company.

Connecting strategy to brand

Walmart's Strategic Vision can be described with Chuck Urtin's favorite word: Simple. It is a high volume, low cost retail chain store. The company strategy follows the simple philosophy of founder Sam Walton: Offer shoppers lower prices than they can get anywhere else.[2]

Walmart delivers its low price promise to its customers in a bold, simple way. For the 19 years prior to 2007, every Walmart posted the word "Always" above the entrance when entering a store. This bold signage underscores founder Sam Walton's promise of "Always Low Prices."

Since 2008, Walmart's new slogan has been "Save Money. Live Better." The low price promise is still there, but now there is an expanded lifestyle appeal. The core strategy, going back to Walton's original customer promise, has never changed.

To assure fulfillment of this low price promise, Walmart took command of its resources. It invested heavily in the technology required to most effectively operate its stores and communicate within the supply chain. The company relentlessly pressured its suppliers, as partners in delivering the promise, to lower their prices or improve product quality. Walmart became the model of efficient operations. The entire Walmart machine was painstakingly designed and optimized for the single purpose of fulfilling its low price commitment. Customers flock to Walmart because of its myriad locations, extended store hours, and wide selection of nearly anything a budget-conscious consumer might want. However, there is one particular thing not expected by Walmart shoppers: An especially intimate customer service experience.

When comparing Walmart's customer experience to, let's say, their direct competitor, Target Corp., the second-largest U.S. discount retailer, or Starbuck's, the largest coffee house company in the world, or even Southwest Airlines, the largest U.S. airline by volume in 2010, Walmart doesn't quite make the grade. The stores aren't quite as clean and perhaps the staff not quite as courteous. If the checkout line gets backed up, well, it gets backed up – until that bottleneck begins to interfere markedly with the brisk flow of commerce. This strategy defies logic, yet Walmart's commitment to its volume-price strategy and brand is so complete that it works. They have built a retail empire around it. They make no claim to being a service leader. They are the price leader. And Walmart's price-driven strategy has made them the biggest company in the world. Its Strategic Vision works because the company lives and breathes Sam Walton's promise of "Always Low Prices."

So what about the little guy? Where I live in Saugerties, New York, there is an independent shoe store in the center of the village called Montano's. In a retailing milieu increasingly dominated by Target, Walmart, and large footwear-specialty chains, running an independent shoe store profitably is no small feat. Montano's ably illustrates how a small retailer can survive and thrive by finding - and leveraging - a differentiating niche.

Family-owned and operated, Montano's was founded in 1906.

Montano's in Saugerties

The sign out front offers a clue as to what makes Montano's special. At the top of the sign you will see "Board Certified Pedorthist" proudly displayed. A Pedorthist is a medical professional who specializes in the use of footwear and supportive devices to address conditions which affect the feet and lower limbs. If you visit Montano's website, owners Ed and Anthony Montano define and proclaim their niche by saying, "We specialize in properly fitted footwear."

In other words, as a Pedorthist, Ed does more than just sell shoes. He specializes in making sure they fit well. On a typical Saturday, Montano's is a busy place. The last time I shopped there, I had three people ahead of me, and every clerk was busy with a customer. At Montano's, customer service centers on a knowledge base about the proper fitting of shoes. Therefore, every sale includes a personal fitting by Ed, Anthony, or a trained associate. The shop owner, and Pedorthist, wants to be sure that everyone leaving his store leaves with "properly fitted footwear." The product selection is extensive, but is also restricted to those brands that Montano's deems as having certain sizing features which enable a proper fit. I once asked why the only brand of athletic shoe sold at Montano's was New Balance. The answer was that it was the only well-known brand which comes in a range of widths acceptable by Montano's standards. Sure enough, my feet have a width that falls between two sizes, and the slightly larger width recommended by Ed was more comfortable for me. This is quite different from buying shoes at a discount department store where a clerk may not even be present and the process of buying shoes is self service. After being in business for over a century, Montano's service-based strategy continues to make money, since it thrives even though there are two Walmarts within eleven miles of the store.

In contrast to Walmart's value model, Ed and Anthony Montano hold their own by delivering an exceptional experience differentiated by their expertise in fitting shoes. It is highly unlikely you will ever see a board certified Pedorthist in a Walmart. The cost of the training, certification, and a premium wage would challenge Walmart's volume-price strategy. Montano's has found a way to succeed in the Walmart age by choosing and committing to a service-driven, not price-driven, Strategic Vision.

We have talked about a big company, Walmart, and a small company, Montano's, each deploying successful strategies with different approaches: One based on high volume and low prices, the other based on exceptional service and higher-quality products. Both succeed because each company is totally committed to their Strategic Visions. They got it right.

What happens when a company gets it wrong?

In the seventies, Xerox dominated the document duplication market with a 90% market share.[3] Its name was synonymous with copying. In those days, people would often ask for a "Xerox" instead of a "copy," sort of like asking for a "Kleenex" instead of a "tissue." By 2006, Xerox market share had declined to 9%[4] in each category of black and white and color printing. Forty years ago, the company was recognized as a leading innovator of a wide range of technologies that are now part of everyday life. Yet today, it is not a player in any of them. What happened?

Looking back at the Xerox strategy in the seventies, its strength was built on a patented dry ink process called xerography.[5] The technology revolutionized office copying and made buckets of money for Xerox. The strategy seemed rock-solid: Based on the superiority of the xerographic process and a scarcity of viable competitors, robust profits were virtually assured. Xerox also had a strong company brand. Along with IBM, Xerox was perceived as one of the era's top innovators, a provider of products which drastically boosted worker productivity. There were no serious competitive threats because rival copy technologies were messy, less reliable, and produced poor quality documents.

With its amazing technology portfolio, throughout the seventies, Xerox dominated the high-volume corporate copy market with its large-capacity models. At the same time, it met the needs of smaller enterprises with affordable, small machines. Xerox equipment was constantly upgraded and new models frequently introduced - hence its astounding 90% market share. With that level of saturation, however, it was becoming increasingly difficult for the company to unlock sales growth in the office copying business alone.

In what seemed like the perfect strategy, the company began moving toward diversification. From its research and development facility in Palo Alto, California, a series of pioneering innovations emerged. Xerox engineers designed the Star workstation, the first computer that incorporated Graphical User Interface (GUI)[6] technology. Today, we all know this as the point-and-click technology behind the computer mouse and touch screen, and Xerox was the first major licensee of the GUI innovation.

Xerox also developed one of the first true personal computers, invented the Ethernet network communications protocol, and successfully mass-marketed the fax machine. In addition, the company dabbled in mainframe computing and went on to pioneer laser imaging technology, which would revolutionize printing and copying on a personal and small-group scale. To provide technical and managerial expertise for its employees, Xerox operated a futuristic training campus in Leesburg, Virginia. With market domination, and a long list of proprietary new technology and innovations, Xerox was poised to continue its remarkable success story.

Not so fast. Xerox never committed to capturing the new market opportunities its extensive investment in research and development was creating. Perhaps, the company's overwhelming success with its copier-machine business clouded its Strategic Vision, leading to the abandonment of several game-changing technologies that, today, are a common part of our lives.

Two events I can recall from back in the 70's demonstrate these missed opportunities. The first was the story about an open house at the Xerox Palo Alto Research Center. Among the guests was Steve Jobs, from Apple Computer, Inc., who was "blinded" when shown the GUI interface. In recounting this first encounter with the technology innovation, Jobs was quoted as saying, "I thought it was the best thing I had ever seen in my life. ... It was obvious to me that all computers would work like this someday."[7] Evidently, Xerox failed to grasp Steve Job's epiphany. Shortly thereafter, Apple incorporated the technology in the Apple Lisa computer. The Lisa evolved into the Apple MacIntosh personal computer, the first easy-to-use PC, which was priced within popular reach. Apple sure knew what to do with the golden egg that Xerox didn't even know it had.

The second event happened when I was working at Xerox's Denver branch office. I still recall being baffled by an executive announcement that Xerox would focus strategically on its large, centralized copier-machine business. In essence, the company all but abandoned the emerging personal computer and network printing technologies. Since the high-volume market was where Xerox was making its money, the company seems to have erroneously decided its unproven technologies were mostly a distraction from its core business.

With that decision, the company cemented a strategy that, looking back today, failed to capitalize on the available opportunities. Over the next few years, the large, high-volume copier market eroded as personal printers and small copiers proliferated. What is left of this market segment today is shared with Konica Minolta Holdings, Inc. and Canon, Inc. And, while most computer owners today own personal printers with network printing, fax, and copier function, few of the machines bear the Xerox nameplate.

So what went wrong? In spite of everything working in its favor, Xerox failed to develop a Strategic Vision for capturing the myriad opportunities its own innovations were generating. In the context of *Solving the Brand Puzzle*, it was a well-managed organization. It had a well-known and respected brand identity. A culture of accountability and professionalism was established throughout the company. The piece of the brand puzzle that was missing was a more forward-thinking Strategic Vision.

From a strategic viewpoint, I can empathize with Xerox. With a long list of innovative "gizmos" potentially offering a bright future, the company nevertheless struggled with ways of bringing its unfamiliar, although labor-saving, new-fangled office products to market. For those of us who like change, innovation is a thrill ride! But innovation is also a very lonely place. Innovators are pioneers. There are no best practices to follow when you're writing the story for the first time. Innovation is also financially risky. Throw in ego battles, risk assessments, and leadership focused on shareholder value, and you're sailing directly into a near-perfect storm. It's easy to see how Xerox could fall into a trap of false security given its market dominance in office copiers.

Today, Xerox paints quite a different picture of its capabilities in a two-minute commercial, on YouTube.com, titled *A World Made Simpler.*[8] In it, Xerox claims to advance humanity with technology. It lists company capabilities that include information sharing, anti-counterfeit packaging, pop-up call centers, simultaneous monitoring of all a doctor's patients, installing cameras on school busses, and reducing the number of cars on the road.

This commercial was a bit confusing to me so I visited Xerox.com seeking clarification. On the "At a Glance" page[9] the company identifies its products and services in this way:

> "For more than a half a century, Xerox has been a leader in document technology and services. We continue to build on this heritage of innovation. Through our acquisition of Affiliated Computer Services, we now are the world's leading enterprise for business process and document management, offering global services from claims reimbursement and automated toll transaction to customer care centers and HR benefits management. The new Xerox is dedicated to innovation, service and giving our customers the freedom to focus on what matters most: Your real business."

I still didn't quite get it. After viewing the commercial and reading the "At A Glance" page on the website, my perception of Xerox's Strategic Vision was that it seems to be building its future on services, not products. Yet, when visiting additional pages in the website, it was obvious that Xerox continues to offer an impressive portfolio of equipment, from small personal printers to large, high volume publishing presses. This appears to be a large part of its core business and is definitely part of its heritage. However, it is not communicated in either the commercial or the "At A Glance" description. Instead, the company emphasizes a complex and diverse list of services which left me wondering what Xerox's Strategic Vision really is.

Maybe the performance of Xerox stock best tells the story. On August 17, 1981, around the time I left Xerox, one share of stock traded for $46.50[10]. Since then, the stock split twice and transformed that single share into six shares. On August 17, 2012, Xerox stock was trading at $7.41. When you do the math, six shares multiplied by the current price of $7.41 turns the value of that single share, worth $46.50 back in 1981, into a value of just $44.46 today.

Let's compare that to another technology giant, IBM. On August 17, 1981, shares of IBM stock were trading at $56.75[11]. On August 17, 2012, the closing price was $201.22. However, over that period of time, IBM stock split twice, transforming the one original share into four shares. The original $56.75 investment now has a value of $804.88.

Developing a Strategic Vision

We have just looked at how Strategic Vision, or the lack of Strategic Vision, has affected several companies. These examples highlight why Strategic Vision is an important piece in solving your brand puzzle.

Developing a Strategic Vision is a four-step process: 1) discovering your brand, 2) establishing the Cornerstones of your brand, 3) exploring the TWSO (threats, weaknesses, strengths, and opportunities) affecting your company, and, 4) forging your Strategic Vision based on the results of the first three steps. Within each of the four steps is a series of exercises that will guide you through the process.

Brand Discovery (Core Values)
    Heritage and Traditions
    Purpose of Business
Brand Cornerstones
    Company Brand Standards
    Staff Behavioral Guidelines
    Customer Brand Statement
    Department Brand Integration
TWSO
    Threats
    Weaknesses
    Strengths
    Opportunities
Strategic Vision
    Statement of Vision
    Strategic Goals

Brand Discovery (Core Values)
  Heritage and Traditions
  Purpose of Business
Brand Cornerstones
  Company Brand Standards
  Staff Behavioral Guidelines
  Customer Brand Statement
  Department Brand Integration
TWSO
  Threats
  Weaknesses
  Strengths
  Opportunities
Strategic Vision
  Statement of Vision
  Strategic Goals

Brand Discovery

Brand Discovery captures a company's heritage and traditions, and defines the true purpose of its business. These elements comprise its core values. It is my belief that a successful Strategic Vision cannot be developed without consideration of a company's core values.

Heritage and Traditions. The first exercise in Brand Discovery is defining the Heritage and Traditions of the organization. Who were the founders and what did they stand for? What motivated them? What leaders, philosophies, and accomplishments brought the organization to the present? Great companies follow great leaders; people like Walt Disney and Sam Walton. Great companies accomplish great things, such as companies like Apple, Disney, and Amazon. Understanding a company's Heritage and Traditions is the foundation of Brand Discovery. It will establish the company's sense of purpose.

Thinking back to Irwin Bank, remember the story about Tobias Berkowitz? During a strategic planning session decades later, at the bank, there wasn't one person who knew the story. The senior managers were plotting the future of the company, yet had no knowledge of its rich heritage. They were no longer connected with the core values established by Irwin Bank's founding fathers. It is my belief that a Strategic Vision should use the company's history as a reference point in planning its future.

Purpose of Business. It is important to answer the question, "What business are you really in?" A well documented example is Starbucks. Shrewdly staying on message, Starbucks' CEO Howard Schultz has repeatedly said that while Starbucks is a coffee company at heart, the company provides "much more than the best cup of coffee—we offer a community gathering place where people come together to connect and discover new things."[12] Although it sells coffee, Starbucks is in the potentially more lucrative "community gathering place" business.

Another example is Disney. Disney provides entertainment in a variety of formats from cinema to theme parks. However, Disney would tell you, "We Create Happiness,"[13] a defining tradition that goes back to 1955, the year Disneyland opened in Anaheim, California. And don't forget Montano's. Montano's sells shoes but is in the business of providing foot comfort. What business are you in?

Brand Cornerstones

Cornerstones define how operations behind-the-scenes affect how you will communicate your brand to the customer. The four Brand Cornerstones that define how your company will operate are:

- Company Brand Standards
- Staff Behavioral Guidelines
- Customer Brand Statement
- Department Brand Integration

Brand Discovery (Core Values)
  Heritage and Traditions
  Purpose of Business
Brand Cornerstones
  Company Brand Standards
  Staff Behavioral Guidelines
  Customer Brand Statement
  Department Brand Integration
TWSO
  Threats
  Weaknesses
  Strengths
  Opportunities
Strategic Vision
  Statement of Vision
  Strategic Goals

From how your staff treats customers to how decisions that affect customers are made, Brand Cornerstones create consistency throughout the entire company. To help you understand why they are so important, let's look at each Cornerstone in greater detail.

Company Brand Standards. Company Brand Standards make up a short, simple list of a company's most essential operational attributes. Because they are listed in order of importance, they create a decision tree which the entire organization can follow.

Disney runs its entire operation on four simple Company Brand Standards (Disney refers to them as "Service Standards"):[14]

- Safety – Nothing is more important than the safety of staff and guests.
- Courtesy – This is Disney's word for customer service.
- Show – Since Disney provides entertainment, everything about the guest experience should be entertaining.
- Efficiency – Profit and cost control are still important, but

not more important than Safety, Courtesy and Show.

At Walt Disney World's Magic Kingdom in Orlando, Florida, the staff enters the park at the opposite end from where guests arrive. Once in proper costume for their "role" as "cast members," they commute by underground tunnel to their proper park location. Disney stresses that it would be bad Show for a princess from *Fantasy Land* to be seen walking through *Tomorrow Land*.

Here is a hypothetical story one Disney Institute program facilitator told me. It demonstrates how an employee would apply the decision tree in a situation of conflict.

Imagine a cast member arriving in *Fantasy Land*. She looks over into *Adventure Land* and spots a child walking precariously along a wall, creating a concern for the child's safety. It would be bad Show for a princess to be seen in *Adventure Land*. What to do? Follow the decision tree! Safety trumps all. Go save the kid, even in an improper costume.

On her way to save the child, a guest stops our princess to ask her to take a family photo. What to do? Follow the decision tree! Safety also trumps Courtesy. Excusing herself from the photo op, our princess proceeds to complete the rescue, returns to the guests to take the photo, and then promptly gets back to her post in *Fantasy Land*. A simple four step process guided a rank and file employee about how to properly manage a complex series of decisions. This demonstrates the effectiveness of Company Brand Standards.

Next, I'd like to share an example of how Irwin Bank developed its Company Brand Standards using the Disney model. We began by comparing ourselves to Disney. What did the two companies have in common and what were differences? Our first conclusion was that we had Safety, Courtesy and Efficiency in common. What about Show? We dropped that one. We weren't entertaining anyone.

Next, we asked ourselves, "What was different about a bank compared to a theme park?" The answer was regulation. Banking is a heavily regulated industry. We had to consider regulations governing privacy, governance, lending, deposits, and money laundering. We broke them down into two categories: Compliance and Confidentiality. We then developed several test scenarios to determine where they would fit in our list of Company Brand Standards.

Obviously, Safety came out on top. Our product, money, is so popular that people with guns try to take it away from us! Safety definitely ruled in banking. Several of us made the argument for Courtesy to be next. We were all committed to customer service. We had just invested a lot of money with Disney Institute to develop our service culture. During the debate, however, someone brought up the fact that regulations restricted the number of times that a customer could access a money market account each month. Compliance was creating a service restriction that was inconvenient to some customers but beyond our control. Compliance trumped Courtesy.

Next, we debated whether Confidentiality was more important than Compliance. Although we placed much effort on keeping customer information private, if a subpoena were to be served for customer records, we would have to comply. That demonstrated that Compliance trumped Confidentiality. And what about Efficiency? We agreed that although we placed emphasis on lowering our cost of operations and managing rates, as a standard, Efficiency was last. If we were to need a camera for safety, we would purchase it without question. However, efficiency would create the accountability to get the best price. Likewise, if we were to need to make a capital investment in software or a new office to improve Courtesy, we would make the investment but within budget guidelines. As with Disney, although Efficiency was last on the decision tree, it nonetheless played a role in the decision-making process.

We were pleased with the conclusion of our exercise. Five simple words now defined Irwin Bank's Company Brand Standards.

- Safety
- Compliance
- Confidentiality
- Courtesy
- Efficiency

We soon had an opportunity to test our decision tree. Irwin Bank's management had determined that it needed new software for its core operations. We interviewed several vendors. After their demonstrations, Chuck Urtin, true to form, said, "Let's make this simple. Let's use our new Company Brand Standards." The top three, Safety, Compliance, and Confidentiality, were easy to evaluate.

Chuck expressed the obvious: If these vendors weren't safe, compliant, and secure, they would not have survived as industry leaders. Therefore, we ranked them as equal in these three categories.

As for Efficiency, prices and the effort to implement were similar from all vendors. The decision came down to Courtesy. Which system would best serve the customer and have the least amount of negative impact? As it turned out, one of the candidate's software used some of the very same interfacing systems already familiar to our customers, including on-line banking and bill payment. Therefore, there would be minimal impact due to the change. An additional benefit was that the same system also offered our customer service staff the most advanced and efficient CRM (Customer Relationship Management) home screen. This made it easier for customer service representatives to identify customers, evaluate their business relationships, and assess customer product needs.

Our Company Brand Standards had guided us to a final decision. The best score in the category of Courtesy won. Our Brand Standards decision tree worked!

Staff Behavioral Guidelines. The second Cornerstone after Company Brand Standards is Staff Behavioral Guidelines: Another simple list of behaviors that explains how employees should engage each customer. The list is not in any particular order; employees are expected to follow all of the guidelines. This assures that customers receive consistent service.

Disney has effectively used Staff Behavioral Guidelines, which it refers to as Service Guidelines, to establish customer service consistency among its 60,000-plus employees throughout its theme parks. The list is frequently displayed behind-the-scenes as an employee reminder. Employees also carry the list on small cards in their wallets. In order to fulfill Disney's promise to "Create Happiness," all employees are expected to demonstrate the behaviors defined in their Service Guidelines.

The Disney Service Guidelines are:
- Make eye contact and smile.
- Greet and welcome each and every guest.
- Seek out guest contact.
- Provide immediate service recovery.

- Display appropriate body language at all times.
- Preserve the "magical" guest experience.
- Thank each and every guest.

Think about the beautiful simplicity of these seven guidelines. The entire staff can align its behavior to them. Hopefully, you are beginning to sense how this will impact consistency in brand delivery.

Customer Brand Statement. The third Cornerstone is the Customer Brand Statement. It states what you do, for whom you do it, and how you do it. The Customer Brand Statement is written to the customer and should answer these questions:

Brand Discovery (Core Values)
  Heritage and Traditions
  Purpose of Business
Brand Cornerstones
  Company Brand Standards
  Staff Behavioral Guidelines
  Customer Brand Statement
  Department Brand Integration
TWSO
  Threats
  Weaknesses
  Strengths
  Opportunities
Strategic Vision
  Statement of Vision
  Strategic Goals

- To whom are you speaking? In other words, who is your customer?
- How do you describe your type of business, and how do you intend to be perceived?
- What specific things does your company do to benefit your customers?
- How do you do it, and why are you unique?

The Brand Statement establishes the company's commitment to the customer and states what the company must live up to. Here is an example of a well-written Brand Statement developed by a financial institution.

> To the citizens and businesses of [market area], we are your trusted and sound financial institution. We make your life easier by providing personal and convenient financial solutions, and a customer experience driven by innovative technology, reliable service, and easy access on which you can rely.

A well-developed Brand Statement is better than the traditional mission statement, because it not only describes the company's intentions, but also incorporates its philosophy.

Department Brand Integration. The fourth and final Corner-

Brand Discovery (Core Values)
   Heritage and Traditions
   Purpose of Business
Brand Cornerstones
   Company Brand Standards
   Staff Behavioral Guidelines
   Customer Brand Statement
   Department Brand Integration
TWSO
   Threats
   Weaknesses
   Strengths
   Opportunities
Strategic Vision
   Statement of Vision
   Strategic Goals

stone is Department Brand Integration. This Cornerstone describes the roles that staff, workplace environment, and operational systems play within each specific department, to ensure that each Company Brand Standard is met.

When Department Brand Integration is complete, it is structured in the format of a grid for each department. *Appendix A* provides an example that demonstrates how the marketing department of a community-based, financial institution formulated its integration grid. The company had already established Safety and Soundness, Compliance, Confidentiality, Member Experience, Convenience, and Efficiency as its Company Brand Standards. Now, it was up to each department to develop its own unique integration grid. Each function and resource in every department had to fulfill a specific Company Brand Standard.

In addition to the marketing department's grid, ten other unique integration grids were completed: one for each department in the company.

TWSO (traditionally known as SWOT)[15]

We discussed Brand Discovery as step one and Brand Cornerstones as step two of the *Solving the Brand Puzzle* Strategic Visioning process. The third step is the examination of TWSO, which stands for Threats, Weaknesses, Strengths, and Opportunities - in that precise order. I believe TWSO offers a more realistic approach, than the commonly accepted SWOT approach, which presents the analytical sequence as Strengths, Weaknesses, Opportunities, and Threats.

Here's why Threats and Weaknesses should come first. Think about this from a hypothetical military viewpoint. Imagine you are the best trained and equipped foot soldier in the world. You and your platoon march into the fight and, instead of an infantry battle, you find yourself up against a tank! Now what are your chances? It sure would have been nice to know more about that Threat before walking into the battle. For all of your Strengths, you are overwhelmed. Had you been aware, you might have avoided the battle or shown up with a rocket launcher. In the context of the traditional SWOT analysis, your Strength, which in your mind was beyond question, was useless against a superior Threat not properly assessed.

The foot soldier's dilemma makes a strong case for changing the order of the SWOT analysis. I believe the first question should not be, "What are you good at?" Instead, it should be, "What Threats keep you awake at night?" That means examining your Threats first, in the order of TWSO, not SWOT.

Threats. The retail industry offers many examples of threat vulnerabilities. When I think about big names that have gone belly-up, here are a few: Consumer electronics giant Circuit City

Brand Discovery (Core Values)
  Heritage and Traditions
  Purpose of Business
Brand Cornerstones
  Company Brand Standards
  Staff Behavioral Guidelines
  Customer Brand Statement
  Department Brand Integration
TWSO
  Threats
  Weaknesses
  Strengths
  Opportunities
Strategic Vision
  Statement of Vision
  Strategic Goals

Stores, Inc.; housewares emporium Linens 'n Things, Inc.; northeast United States discount department store Jamesway; home improvement warehouse concept pioneer Builders Square; and discount electronics chain Crazy Eddie. Department store fallen flags include B. Altman, a New York classic, plus Kaufmann's and Horne's, two venerable Pittsburgh retailing landmarks. How about an entire retail category? Catalog showrooms. Gone. In fact, hundreds of retail, restaurant, and specialty retail chains have disappeared over the past 15 or 20 years.

Blockbuster once dominated the movie rental industry. Today they are closing stores as they fight to survive. At its peak, Blockbuster owned or franchised about 4,000 freestanding stores[16] employing nearly 60,000 people. In September, 2010, the company filed for Chapter 11 Bankruptcy protection and soon announced a plan to close 900 of its remaining 3,000 stores.[17]

Where did Blockbuster's strategy fail? It's easy to critique the business model today. Just look at the market. Why would anyone make two round trips to a video store when movies can be delivered to the mailbox or downloaded from online sources? Better yet, why wait for the mail when the cable company, Amazon, Netflix, and other providers, will stream them to you instantly? Could Blockbuster's strategy have anticipated these trends ten years ago? Could it be that the company's Strength as the overwhelming market leader clouded its assessment of Threats looming on the horizon?

A Walmart spokesman named Tom Williams described his company's situational-awareness imperative by saying, "We seem to do best when we are constantly looking over our shoulder."[18] That statement shows a lot of respect for Threat assessment, a valued part of Walmart's culture. Why does Walmart constantly "look over its shoulder?"[18] Because respecting competitive Threats – and addressing them immediately – is how it continues to crank out huge profits every minute of every day and remain on top.

Here is an example of how Walmart assessed a Threat and turned it into an opportunity. Although the company dominated retail sales in its stores, it recognized the Threat from the emerging online shopping trend. It established itself online not only with general merchandise, but also with online specialties like music downloads. Walmart was not going to be left behind. As in sports, a strong offense starts with solid defense.

In Jim Collins' book *Good to Great: Why Some Companies Make the Leap... and Others Don't*, one of the companies profiled was Circuit City. The electronics-retailer once seemed to do almost everything right. During a 15-year period, starting in the early eighties, Circuit City out-performed the general stock market growth by 18 times. Yet in 2009, the company was liquidated.[19] What happened? Circuit City underestimated the Threat posed by Amazon.com and Walmart's rapid push into the consumer electronics segment.[20]

Here is another example. At different moments in history, both K-Mart and Sears Roebuck and Company each held the distinction of being the world's largest retail store chain. Where are they today? Remember Walmart's $375 billion in sales reported in calendar year 2008? Sears Holdings, which is today the parent company of both K-Mart and Sears, reported revenue of $50 billion for the same period, and year-over-year, same-store sales[21] on the aggregate were declining by almost 5%. Walmart's annual sales are now generating about seven times the revenue of K-Mart and Sears combined. Hopefully by now you're getting the point: A company cannot afford to ignore Threats just because it is enjoying success.

Weaknesses, Strengths, and Opportunities. Now that you understand what Threats you are up against, it's time to analyze your organization for Weaknesses, Strengths, and Opportunities. While the Threat assessment still has you hiding under your desk in the fetal position, now is the time to look internally.

Good news! By looking at your Threats list, you can more easily identify your Weaknesses, Strengths, and Opportunities. That's the beauty of starting with a Threats analysis.

For example: How aware are you of the business environment? If you do not understand your competition, economic conditions, market and customer demographic data, and changing trends, then that's Weakness. But if you do, then you have Strength.

Brand Discovery (Core Values)
Heritage and Traditions
Purpose of Business
Brand Cornerstones
Company Brand Standards
Staff Behavioral Guidelines
Customer Brand Statement
Department Brand Integration
TWSO
Threats
Weaknesses
Strengths
Opportunities
Strategic Vision
Statement of Vision
Strategic Goals

Moving forward, your awareness of your Threats, Weaknesses, and Strengths now equips you to capture realistic Opportunities. Should you be opening new stores? Expanding product offerings? Lowering prices? Improving customer service? Engaging in the TWSO process will help you face the facts and develop meaningful actions. In the end, you will have a more realistic and effective Strategic Vision.

A brainstorming guide to the TWSO exercise

Conduct a TWSO exercise annually with this attitude:
- Be defensive
- Respect the competition
- Embrace innovation
- Welcome change

Probe the following topics in depth as they apply to each of the

TWSO categories.

Environmental:
- Economic conditions
- Changing demographics
- Changing lifestyles

Competition:
- Existing and emerging competitors
- Unlikely competitors
- Emerging technologies
- New and better products
- Lower prices
- Innovation

Internal operations:
- Management/board alignment
- Management competency
- Staff competency
- Products
- Operational efficiency
- Sufficient customer data
- Sufficient market intelligence
- Branding integrity
- Leadership ego
- "Good ol' Boys" culture
- Risk management vulnerabilities
- Capital strength
- Technology

Strategic Vision

With your Brand Discovered, Cornerstones established, and TWSO defined, you now have the foundation on which to create your Strategic Vision. After all the work you've done, it will all come down to one simple document. At the top will be your Statement of Vision. Beneath that will be a list of Strategic Goals validating that your Statement of Vision is achievable. Let's talk about how the Statement of Vision and Strategic Goals work together.

Using your renewed understanding of your organization's brand, the Statement of Vision should express what you want your company to accomplish in the future. It should present the "big picture" by including topics such as market share, overall growth, innovation, and brand. Strategic Goals define what your company needs to do in order to fulfill that Statement of Vision. For example, if your Statement of Vision includes market share as a topic, then you should list specific goals which support that topic. These might include specifics about product innovation, use of technology, and pricing structure.

Brand Discovery (Core Values)
  Heritage and Traditions
  Purpose of Business
Brand Cornerstones
  Company Brand Standards
  Staff Behavioral Guidelines
  Customer Brand Statement
  Department Brand Integration
TWSO
  Threats
  Weaknesses
  Strengths
  Opportunities
Strategic Vision
  Statement of Vision
  Strategic Goals

A note of caution: It is during the process of developing a Strategic Vision that many companies fall into the trap of creating a Statement of Vision that is unachievable. Think back to the Montano's story. The shoe store is located in a small town within ten miles of two Walmarts. In addition, there are at least four other specialty shoe stores in the area. Would it make sense for Montano's to claim this Statement of Vision: "To be the market leader in shoe sales in the northeastern US?" Of course not. The Strategic Goals required for achieving the amount of growth necessary to fulfill that statement would be unrealistic. It's highly unlikely that Montano's would be able to marshal the capital, infrastructure, and expertise needed to dominate shoe sales in its local market, let alone the entire northeast. It makes more sense for Montano's to scale its Statement of Vision back to reality and focus on the store's niche of expertly-fitted footwear.

Let's flip it around to Walmart. What if Walmart were to come up with a really bold Statement of Vision such as, "To be the price leader and dominant food and merchandise retailer by volume in North America," would that be appropriate? You bet! It may sound like bravado, but coming from the largest company in the world, it would be a very realistic statement. When writing its Strategic Goals, Walmart would already know it possesses the supply chain, logistics, technology, and retail store infrastructure needed to pull it off.

As stated earlier, every company's Strategic Vision is unique. A realistic and practical Strategic Vision is the payoff for the effort invested in Brand Discovery, establishing Cornerstones, and exploring TWSO. Strategic Vision defines *where you want your organization to go*. In the next chapter, you will see how this is critical to management's ability to define the tactical plan that maps out *how to get there*.

See *Appendix A* for a step-by-step case study demonstrating how one company discovered its brand and established Brand Cornerstones.

That's a wrap

There is a sequel to the Carol Burnett story. I'll call it "Ten Minutes in Carol Burnett's Kitchen." When my work was complete at the Hamilton residence, I politely asked Ms. Burnett if she would autograph a publicity photo for me. She apologized that she was out of them but invited me back to her home the following Saturday and she would gladly provide one at that time. Now, how many people get a personal invitation to visit a celebrity at home? I gladly accepted! On Saturday, I returned with my fiancée and Carol graciously provided us with an autographed photo. As we prepared to leave, a yellow Rolls Royce convertible, California license plate JN1, pulled into the driveway. Up to the kitchen door strolled Jim Nabors, popular at the time for his television roles as the dim-witted, but lovable, gas-station attendant Gomer Pyle on *The Andy Griffith Show* and as the star of *Gomer Pyle - USMC*. It was Carol's birthday and her good friend, Jim Nabors, was there to offer a birthday wish. As a humble Beverly Hills cable guy I watched in awe, feeling just a bit out of place in Joe and Carol's kitchen, in the middle of this high-wattage, impromptu birthday celebration. Great customer service builds great opportunities and also provided me with a priceless Hollywood moment.

Thank you, Carol. I still cherish the photo!

Photo autographed by Carol Burnett. "Beep" was my cable TV nickname.

CHAPTER 3

Management

MARTA and the Ritz

For as many times as I had travelled through the Hartsfield-Jackson Atlanta International Airport, I had never been to downtown Atlanta. My first visit was in the spring of 2010 when I attended a conference at the Ritz-Carlton hotel. As I walked through the terminal, I noticed directional signs labeled "MARTA," the Metropolitan Atlanta Rapid Transit Authority. MARTA operates the rail and bus system in Atlanta. I am a rail enthusiast, so the possibility of using commuter rail for the trip downtown interested me. However, the signs in the airport terminal were not clear as to whether or not there was a stop near the Ritz-Carlton. I checked in a pamphlet without success. I looked for an information booth. No luck. Finally, I gave up and took a cab. MARTA's sign program had failed me.

My stay at the Ritz-Carlton, as expected, was excellent. The 5-star hotel provided a great room, comfortable bed, excellent food, and fabulous staff. My entire three day visit was a rewarding customer experience. But then, that's understandable because the Ritz-Carlton is known for world-class customer service, right up there with Disney.

I was enjoying my Ritz-Carlton experience when, at some point during my stay, I looked out of my hotel room window and spotted a small building right across the street labeled "MARTA." It appeared that there was a rail stop next to the hotel after all. How convenient! I could take the train back to the airport. Being a train buff, I know quite a bit of railroad history and have a good-sized collection of model trains. I like to ride trains, watch trains, and even chase trains. So, when this opportunity to ride on the MAR-TA became evident, I was excited about taking my first ride.

I was feeling good about the value, too. The concierge at the Ritz-Carlton told me the fare would be just $2 to the airport. After spending $32 plus tip for cab transport, this was a real bargain.

Upon checking out of the hotel, I crossed the street and headed for the building I had seen from my room. As I walked up to it, I could not see a door. I walked around to the next side of the building. No door there either. I walked around back, and still no entrance. It was then that I spotted a small news stand where I asked how to take the train. The vendor pointed over his shoulder to the other side of the street. I looked across the street and saw a small structure sort of tucked into the streetscape. In fact, the entrance was so minimal I had walked right by it and not seen it.

I crossed the street and entered the station. With my first impression being that it was hard to find, my second impression was that it seemed dark. I looked up at the lights and realized half the fluorescent tubes were burned out. The lack of brightness, in a new and strange environment, created an eerie sense of gloom. After purchasing my fare, I proceeded down a very long escalator into the bowels of MARTA. There I encountered more burned out lights. A second escalator brought me to the large platform. Adding to my growing apprehension was a new sensory input…quiet. I was in a cavernous underground train station; it was practically silent; and only a handful of passengers were waiting. Was there some hidden reason why more people weren't riding the MARTA? It felt like a scene from a Stephen King novel, or an episode of the old TV series, *The Twilight Zone*.

With a sense of relief, I heard the train arriving five minutes later. After boarding, I sat alone at one end of the car while only three other riders sat at the other end. As we entered the next station I noticed it, too, had many burned-out light bulbs. When the train emerged from the underground onto the surface, it felt like we'd entered an urban warfare scene from a video game. Endless graffiti blighted the view from every angle. The train route went through mostly bad neighborhoods and industrial areas, with fences and roofs topped by barbed wire. I was riding the terror train! At first I couldn't find it. Now I couldn't wait to get off it!

I recall my only positive memory of the ride was when the train stopped at one of the stations and a uniformed MARTA cop boarded my car. He sat across the aisle from me. Whew! I had an armed guard. Although he was the first I had seen on the railroad, I was happy to have the good fortune of his presence in my car as more graffiti and barbed wire passed by outside. With a sense of relief, I got off the train when it finally arrived at the airport. The experience left me thinking about an old, sarcastic saying from a depression-era cartoon that read, "What a way to run a railroad!"[1]

Walking out of the Ritz and then riding the MARTA had been, for me, brand culture shock. When I stated earlier that *Solving the Brand Puzzle* is for everyone, I wasn't joking. Why not a railroad? Just because it is run by a government agency doesn't mean it should be exempt from delivering safe, reliable, and comfortable service. What brand standards would apply to a railroad? Safety? Absolutely. Courtesy? You bet! Efficiency? Critical! Commuter railroads are publicly funded. Taxpayers should demand a return for their investment.

Efficient use of taxpayer funds at MARTA should be high on the list of strategic goals, just like making money should be for a commercial business. Delivering a safe ride, beginning with clean, well-kept facilities and equipment, would be another reasonable strategic goal. If the railroad were to achieve the second goal, it would attract more riders, and therefore generate more fare revenue. In doing so, it would create less dependency on the taxpayers and effectively achieve the first goal. My experience with MARTA appeared to indicate a management opportunity. Here are some clues as to why:

- **Marketing.** The sign program at the airport was unclear as to where I could find the train and where it made stops. I found myself wondering how, for a first time rider, a subway station in downtown Atlanta could be so hard to find. With a responsibility to fill the trains and minimize the taxpayer burden, the communication of locations and service quality should be loud and clear. MARTA has signs, but not enough of them in the right places. Management should conduct surveys that would provide feedback on rider perception in order to discover possible improvements in signage.

- **Safety.** The gloomy atmosphere of a poorly illuminated underground rail station does not project an image of safety. Rather, it creates a sense of danger. Is money so tight at MARTA that it can't afford light bulbs? It made me wonder if that's the case, maybe the entire system is unsafe! The stations were built with plenty of light fixtures but it is up to management to ensure that the burned-out bulbs are replaced.

- **Design.** The train runs through some areas of Atlanta that appear to be unsafe. Mile after mile of scenery dominated by graffiti and barbed wire doesn't exactly make a person feel secure. Surely, the designers could have anticipated the perception of danger that would come from the view out the train's windows! Should barriers and evergreen foliage have been part of the system design?

- **Efficiency.** If the argument against adding more cops and more light bulbs comes down to funding, let's be realistic. I spent two bucks to get to the airport vs. 32 bucks for a cab. If my fare had been double, I wouldn't have thought twice about it!

A 2010 study published by The University of California at Berkeley[2] provides an operational comparison of America's commuter rail systems. When I analyzed annual costs, revenue, and ridership, the data indicated that MARTA generated less revenue per passenger trip than most of its peers. By dividing fare revenues by the number of passenger trips (a trip being defined as one passenger boarding one train), MARTA generated 59 cents in revenue-per-passenger trip. In contrast, the Bay Area Rapid Transit (BART, San Francisco area) generated $2.67; the Washington Metro, $1.59; the Massachusetts Bay Transportation Authority (MBTA, Boston area), $1.03; and the nations' largest, the Metropolitan Transit Authority (MTA, New York City) generated 89 cents per trip. (These revenue calculations factor in monthly passes, discount programs, and multiple trips required to reach a destination. This is why the results show lower revenues-per-trip than the basic fares published by the railroads.)

Although the railroads generate revenue, they do not generate profit. Public transportation systems operate at a loss, which is why they are taxpayer subsidized. If they were not, then far fewer people would use them because fares would be significantly higher. However, what the public gets for its investment goes far beyond a train ride. For example, commuters save on auto expenses while road congestion and air pollution are reduced.

Looking at the deficit-per-trip statistics in the Berkeley study, and comparing them to the revenue-per-trip above, MARTA's loss/revenue ratio per-trip was greater than many of its peers. For its $4.21 in loss, it only generated 59 cents in revenue per trip. BART, on the other hand, lost $4.26 against $2.67 in revenue per trip; Washington's METRO lost $3.44 compared to $1.59; and Boston's MBTA lost $1.95 compared to $1.03. Lastly, New York's MTA lost $1.45 per trip, but generated 89 cents in revenue. These losses were paid for by taxpayers.

The comparisons seem to indicate a reasonable opportunity for MARTA to raise fares and still be a low cost provider. Doing so would provide more value for taxpayers by generating additional income for MARTA. It would also improve the riders' perception of value by funding improvements to the rider experience MARTA delivers.

I have ridden these other railroads and never experienced a sense of danger as I did while riding the MARTA. Even the nation's largest subway system in New York City has done a noteworthy job cleaning up graffiti on its trains, cleaning up stations, and increasing the presence of security police.

Management's opportunity to boost MARTA's brand acceptance seems to be in raising revenue with a fare increase. Sometimes, you just have to raise your price. As we said earlier, every strategy should include making money. At MARTA, if fares were increased, the railroad could improve its sign program, replace more light bulbs, hire more cops, and take steps to block out sightlines to the graffiti. Improving the riders' experience would most likely attract more riders and further increase revenue. That would be a better way to run a railroad!

The critical role of Management

MANAGEMENT

As we established in Chapter 2, once the strategic plan is developed, Management must move it forward for implementation. Strategy is the responsibility of those who must execute it: The Management team. It is up to them to build and execute a tactical plan that includes measurable goals. Most important, their commitment to implementing the strategy requires an all-or-nothing attitude.

Leadership
Tactical Plan
Goals
Scorecard
Staff

One of my mentors, Ron Peduzzi, was a retired high school principal and a Colonel in the United States Marine Corps. He put it to me this way: "Marines are no different than anybody else when it comes to planning how to execute a campaign. We get in a room and argue and debate a plan like everyone else. But when the final decision is made, by God, we are ALL Marines. So whether we agree completely with the plan or not, we go and take that hill!"

Executing a company strategy should be no different. To be successful, the commitment of the Management team is essential. Top leaders must motivate mid-level leaders. Mid-level leaders must motivate first-line leaders. First-line leaders must motivate the rank and file. Any break in the chain creates a threat to success. In *Good to Great*, Jim Collins talks about getting the right people on the bus. In other words, a company needs every level of Management to be committed to the Strategic Vision and capable of executing it. Not every manager is going to agree with every aspect of a complex plan, but they must commit 100% to its implementation. It's like an ongoing military campaign and takes a Marine-like, unified, and structured Management approach to deliver results.

In the context of *Solving the Brand Puzzle*, Management is the force that must run the organization by conforming to the Brand Standards and Strategic Vision. At the same time, Management must uphold the Brand Cornerstones. And, finally, Management should have a comprehensive system to monitor and measure results.

Tying it all together

Now that we have discovered (or re-discovered) our Brand, our Business Purpose, our Brand Cornerstones, and we have a Strategic Vision, wouldn't it make sense to come up with a simple way to integrate all the big pieces into one focused management tool? A balanced scorecard is such a tool[3].

The concept of a scorecard is not new and has widespread popularity. A scorecard is a performance management tool used to track and monitor the execution and consequences of staff activity. It is a list of the Strategic Goals and their periodically updated, measurable results.

When formulating Strategic Goals, I highly recommend referring to the company's Brand Standards. They provide guidance, purpose, and validation. They also help keep the strategic planners and management team engaged with the organization's brand to assure consistency from top to bottom.

How departments make a difference

Individual departments impact the scorecard results in different ways. Therefore, I recommend that each department develop its own individual scorecard based on the company scorecard. This will define and measure how each department's activities will best support the company strategy. Assuming that Brand Standards were considered when the company scorecard was developed, they will now also be a consistent consideration in the operations of every department.

For example, at a financial institution, the entire company may have a goal to increase loan growth. To this end, the marketing department is tasked with bringing in the loans, while the lending department is tasked with processing them. Each department can use its own scorecard guide to associate its role with results. Both departments may share responsibility for the overall result. The marketing department may specifically measure the return on investment (ROI) on the marketing dollars invested, while the lending department may want to focus on underwriting quality and turnaround time.

Scorecard tactical goals should cascade down to individual employees as performance goals. Everyone's actions and performance affect scorecard results and brand execution. In this way, every employee becomes accountable. This process connects the dots between the Strategic Vision and each individual employee.

It eventually comes down to people

After a company has established a process to develop, manage, and measure a plan to achieve its Strategic Vision, it's time to look at the human factors. Are the managers and staff committed to the plan? It would be a shame if, after everything the company has accomplished, everyone were to just shrug their shoulders and refuse to embrace the change. Jim Collins said it best in *Good to Great*: "Get the right people on the bus, the wrong people off the bus, and the right people in the right seats."[4]

Change is not always popular. When Disney first implemented its Service Excellence program, they experienced a significant leadership turnover. Likewise, with an initiative as bold as *Solving the Brand Puzzle*, emphasis must always be placed on hiring and keeping competent and committed individuals, and letting go those who are resisting the change.

Most managers know who their good, mediocre, and poor performers are. But how does a manager determine who is "on the bus?" One way is to rate them on their level of competence and engagement. Here is an Evaluation Guide that may help.

Competent and Engaged. In the Evaluation Guide, competence describes level of expertise, and engagement refers to attitude. Employees who are competent and en-

Evaluation Guide

ENGAGED	
not competent but engaged	competent and engaged
not competent not engaged	competent but not engaged

COMPETENT

gaged are the cream of the crop. They are the company's greatest human assets. Challenge them, reward them, and get them prepared for more responsibility.

Not Competent and Not Engaged. On the other end of the scale are those who are neither competent nor engaged. Face it. These folks have to go. You will never fix them, and they are draining your time and energy. There is a time, as someone from Disney Institute once told me, for these employees to "find their happiness elsewhere."

Remaining are the other two blocks on the evaluation guide that comprise the majority of your employees. Some of this group have great potential to improve. Others are marginal at best and will never be more than that. Let's take a closer look.

Engaged But Not Competent. Engaged but not competent employees can be the most rewarding to work with. When managing them, the goal is to guide them to success. If employees are engaged, often they can be trained to improve their skills or can be moved to a better-suited position.

I once inherited a copywriter; I'll call her Kim. She couldn't write to save herself. She had 15 years' tenure, had held a range of different jobs in the company, but had little natural talent and no formal training as a writer. She had been placed in the job to fill an opening without consideration for her potential for success. Kim was a square peg in a round hole.

Kim had a positive attitude and was a very hard worker. When discussing Kim's performance challenges with her, she agreed with my assessment. She readily admitted that the department demanded a higher level of expertise than she could provide. I suggested that perhaps she should consider moving into an outside sales position. Kim became excited about the new opportunity because she had a tremendous amount of product knowledge, a great attitude, and a wonderful personality. The move proved to be a good fit for Kim, who went on to enjoy her new position with renewed enthusiasm and success. Her sales performance rapidly evolved to outstanding, even noteworthy. In Kim's case, her level of engagement established her as an asset to the organization. As her manager, I had been able to guide her toward a different job – one where she was more competent. It was a win-win for Kim and the company.

Competent But Not Engaged. I have been managing creative staffs for over 25 years. One bright and talented designer, who we will call Dave, came to us with a degree from a top design school. I loved his work, but he was a prima-donna. As Dave's time with the company progressed, he became increasingly difficult to manage.

Our company's brand was built on quality work delivered on time and on budget. However, Dave felt that our customers' budgets and deadlines were an obstruction to his creative expression. I continually tried to coach Dave back to reality, with little success. He paid no attention to either his performance appraisal or my growing concerns. In spite of Dave's competence, his attitude caused him to be disengaged.

While I greatly admire the creative spirit, I also demand that my staff act professionally. One day, Dave elected to take his attitude to a new level by directing the "F" word at me. In my world, this is a clear violation of professional standards, so I responded immediately with an "F" word of my own: Fired!

Dave found out the hard way that his role in brand implementation started with his own professional behavior. For all his talent and ability, he chose to not be engaged. Sadly, as hard as you try to move people to the top category, sometimes they choose the bottom instead.

Solving the Brand Puzzle is not a book about managing people. However, people are the most important part of every organization, and how they are managed ultimately affects the brand.

Strategic Vision and Management are the foundation

How well a company runs is up to the management team. Assuming the first puzzle piece, Strategic Vision, is in place, Management now takes on the critical business of executing the strategy. The importance of Management cannot be overstated. Its success not only determines company performance, but also brand perception. Ultimately, these two behind-the-scenes puzzle pieces create the foundation for what comes next: The customer-facing pieces of Culture and Sensory Experience.

CHAPTER 4

Culture

The Fish Run

Acompany's Culture is defined by the products and services it sells, its philosophy and desire for excellence, and its employees' skills and behaviors. Its commitment to Culture affects *everything*, from consistency of product quality, to level of service, and ultimately, customer satisfaction. What does a culture of excellence look like?

Ask Bob, who ran a seafood restaurant in Connecticut. As manager, making sure his seafood was fresh was paramount. To assure freshness, Bob ordered small quantities of fish several times during the week. He figured out how much to order by factoring in sales history, weather forecasts, holidays, and gut feel. Usually Bob's system worked just fine, but sometimes, things didn't go according to plan.

One Saturday, Bob's restaurant was unusually busy, experiencing an unexpected influx of guests. As a result, his supply of fresh fish was running low. Bob called other seafood restaurant managers he knew across Connecticut, hoping to buy extra fish from them. Unfortunately, they were running low on fish, too. It soon became apparent that no one was going to have enough fish to make it through the weekend. The last fresh fillet would be served well before closing time on Sunday. Not good. Sundays were typically busy, and Bob was concerned about maintaining his restaurant's excellent reputation for fresh seafood. Unfortunately, getting an emergency order of fresh fish on a weekend was difficult because his supplier was closed. However, Bob did have the supplier's cell phone number. Maybe they could work something out. It was worth a try.

Luckily, the supplier answered his phone and Bob explained his predicament. Would the salesman be able to get someone to the warehouse so Bob could get some fish? The reputation of his restaurant was at stake. By now it was Saturday evening, but Bob was told that arrangements would be made for Sunday morning. Fantastic!

Bob called the other restaurants to share the good news. A relay was arranged for Sunday morning. Bob would go to the wholesale supplier and get a shipment of fish. He would then rendezvous with one of the other restaurant managers, who would in turn take a supply to a third restaurant on his way back. Bob would then head for his own store and, along the way, drop off another supply to a fourth restaurant.

So, early Sunday, Bob headed for the seafood supplier. Two stops and 100 miles later, Bob completed the fish run. His restaurant, and three others across the state, had fresh fish for their Sunday guests because Bob was willing to go the extra mile, or in this case 100 miles, in the name of customer satisfaction. Bob's extra effort exemplified a culture of excellence in customer service at his restaurant.

Now, you might think that only a local restaurant owner would care that much about his customers. What makes this story special, though, is that Bob's restaurant, and the other three in the story, are Red Lobster restaurants. Red Lobster is a brand of Darden, the world's largest, full-service restaurant company. Headquartered in Florida, Darden owns and operates 1,900 restaurants, employs approximately 180,000 people worldwide[1], and serves more than 400 million meals a year. In addition to Red Lobster, Darden also operates Olive Garden, Longhorn Steakhouse, Bahama Breeze, Seasons 52, and The Capital Grille. Bob's fish run reflects the culture achieved by a company that is among the top 30 employers in America. It demonstrates how a well-designed corporate culture motivates employees to go above and beyond, every day, to deliver the highest level of customer satisfaction.

Darden has one mission statement for all of its restaurants: "To nourish and delight everyone we serve."[2] Short, sweet, and in this case, spot on. Without fresh fish, Red Lobster fails to "nourish and delight everyone." Just how deep is Darden's culture and how does it inspire a fish run? To answer this question, let's take a closer look at some factors that make up Darden's culture across all its brands.

Guest experience. Darden customers are referred to as guests. The guest experience at a Darden restaurant is a combination of atmosphere, service, menu, and price. At Olive Garden, for example, the atmosphere is casual and comfortable. The server always greets guests with a bottle of wine. I once asked an Olive Garden manager if offering wine, when seating a guest, boosted wine sales. He answered, "Not necessarily," and went on to explain that meals in Italy are always enjoyed with a bottle of wine. This action is a small touch but one that adds to the authenticity of the experience. Selling the wine is not as important as making sure it is offered.

The Olive Garden menu is a unique blend of pastas, meats and classic Italian dishes. Senior chefs are trained in Italy at the Olive Garden Culinary Institute of Tuscany, where they learn the secrets of developing great Italian dishes. Rotating promotional offerings supplement the regular menu and create new reasons to dine at Olive Garden without having to offer discounts. Reasonable prices and generous portions provide a sense of value for the product and overall experience.

Service is carefully structured for consistency throughout Darden's portfolio of restaurants. At Red Lobster, Bob explained to me why I once had to wait at the bar for a table when there were empty tables in the restaurant. The answer was that at Red Lobster, each server is assigned only three tables. Red Lobster has determined that with more than three tables, a server cannot extend optimal service to guests. On a day when the restaurant might be caught short-staffed, Red Lobster does not want guests to think the service is bad. According to Bob, Red Lobster's guests are more tolerant of a before-dinner wait in the lobby, or at the bar, than at their table, where they expect timely service.

Staff. Servers at Red Lobster are not referred to as waitresses and waiters. They are introduced to guests as "seafood experts." Their educational training includes where the seafood comes from, how

Red Lobster controls its quality, methods of preparation, and even directions for shelling a lobster.

Servers must pass a yearly test on their seafood knowledge before being allowed to serve guests. They are given very specific instructions on how to greet guests, garnish meals, and present menu items. And, to achieve consistency, it's the Darden way or the highway.

Consistent with the Disney philosophy that satisfied employees result in satisfied customers, and satisfied customers bring in profits, Darden offers impressive employee benefits and strives for a positive work environment. When quizzed on the job and company, the typical response from employees who have made Red Lobster their career focus is, "I love it here." It is very much like working for Disney. Although pay is average, the staff gets great benefits, plus a considerate working environment. They are given stringent behavioral guidelines, but they are well-trained. And they are apparently mostly satisfied. In 2011, Darden was ranked by *Fortune Magazine* as one of the top 100 companies for which to work. Of all companies that made the grade, Darden was the largest with 167,000 full-time U.S. employees.[3]

Food supply. Food quality and consistency are an important part of Darden's culture. At any Olive Garden across the country, for instance, guests know they'll receive the same flavors, textures, and quality. In order to achieve this level of consistency, Darden manages its complex supply chain through its own subsidiary, Darden Direct Distribution, Inc. This involves a network of direct vendors as well as dedicated distribution centers operated by major restaurant industry suppliers such as Conklin, New York-based Maines Paper, and Food Service, Inc. Maines, for example, provides canned ingredients, spices, cleaning products, and disposable utensils, among its vast array of products and services.

Environmental responsibility. At Red Lobster, guests may ask why a particular species of fish, say swordfish or tuna, cannot be found on the menu. Servers are trained to explain Darden's culture of environmental responsibility. Here is how Red Lobster explains it on their web site:

"Partnering with organizations like the National Fisheries Institute and the Global Aquaculture Alliance, Red Lobster is committed to helping protect the sustainability of the world's seafood supply. We refuse to serve endangered or over-fished species, such as Chilean sea bass, and participate in conservation efforts like never selling live lobsters that are larger than four pounds."[4]

Consistent with this commitment, swordfish and tuna are considered over-fished and therefore are not on Red Lobster's menu.

Red Lobster also serves "farmed" seafood from several countries. Here is Red Lobster's commitment[5] in regard to aquaculture:

"Our seafood only comes from certified, sustainable farms. We require our suppliers to be certified by the Aquaculture Certification Council [that their fish have been] produced according to Best Aquaculture Practices as established by the Global Aquaculture Alliance."[6]

Considering everything we just discussed as the foundation of Darden's culture, we can begin to understand the consistency of the Darden brand. It doesn't matter where you are when you visit a Darden restaurant. Every restaurant looks, feels, and provides tastes just like the one near home.

Think of how things have changed! Large companies like Darden have established a corporate Culture that assures brand integrity, and small businesses are now competitively pressured to keep up. Prior to this turn-of-events, there was a popular assumption that a big company was not able to compete with the quality and service provided by a small, local business. That myth still survives in the minds of some today. However, having learned a lot about Darden's attention to detail and procedures, I would say there is an argument to be made in favor of the ability of a well-run chain to achieve cultural superiority.

Compounding the challenge to smaller restaurateurs, many other large restaurant operators, including Texas Roadhouse, Applebee's, and Ruby Tuesday, have successfully mimicked the Darden model with innovative concepts of their own. When large companies get it right, the loyalty they earn from customers inevitably threatens the mom-and-pop shop.

The meaning of Culture

CULTURE

In the *Solving the Brand Puzzle* formula, Strategic Vision and Management are the behind-the scenes pieces of the complete puzzle. Culture and Sensory Experience are the customer-facing puzzle pieces that affect one's impression of the brand.

Culture is communicated by the product and services as well as the skill and behavior of employees. These elements drive customer satisfaction, repeat business, and referrals. Culture determines your customers' impressions and establishes brand perception in their minds. If you remember only one thing from reading *Solving the Brand Puzzle*, this should be it: **"Your brand is not what *YOU* think it is. It's what your *CUSTOMERS* perceive it to be."**

Elements of Culture
  Philosophy
  Products
  Services
  Behaviors
  Actions
  Skills
  Consistency
  Assessment
  Measurement

Once, at a banking conference, I was shown a chart that depicted the results of an insightful survey. In this survey, hundreds of financial institutions and their customers had been asked a number of questions designed to probe whether the financial institutions really understood what their customers wanted. The heading on the chart that reads, "What the customer desires in a relationship," represents what the customers want their relationship to be with their financial institution. "What the Financial Institution provides," represents the reality of how the financial institutions view the same relationships. *See the results on the next page.*

What a Culture gap! In the first category of answers, it is apparent that the customers desired an empathetic relationship, but the financial institutions wanted operational efficiency. In the second category, the customers said they wanted advice, but the financial institutions wanted sales. The last category says it all. Customers wanted relationships, but the financial institutions wanted profit generators.

The very last line of the chart is my favorite: Customers only wanted a reason to stay. The financial institutions only wanted to make it difficult for customers to leave. By getting customers to

The Customer Relationship Gap

What the customer *desires* in a relationship		What the financial institution *provides*
Flexible and Growing		**A Manufactured Process**
Emotional		Functional
Understanding		Transactional
Flexible	**vs.**	Speedy and efficient
Reciprocal		One-way
Reassuring		Regulated, legislation-focused
Proactive		Reactive
Relevant Solutions		**Pushing Products and Services**
Providing advice, help, and education	**vs.**	Bundling of products and services
Consultative		Selling
Connected and Engaged		**Serviced and Entangled**
Valued and appreciated		Viewed as revenue generators
Known and recognized		Treated as a number, but with a smile
Trust earned over time	**vs.**	Loyalty measured by number of transactions
Woo me with service		Wow them with products
Make me want to stay		Make it difficult to leave

open more accounts and use more services, financial institutions manage to complicate the relationship to the point where it is just too much trouble for the customer to leave. I can't tell you how many times I have heard bankers or their suppliers talk about making their customer relationships "sticky," which means, cross-selling customers into a bunch of different products and services. This makes switching to a competitor such a hassle that they are reluctant to do it. How's that for a "great" marketing strategy? Use inconvenience to force loyalty and hold customers hostage! Ironically, the customer is begging for the nurturing and reliable relationship that the financial institutions superficially allege they want to provide.

So often, the company's internal focus and operational mindset prevent it from engaging the relationship. The customer, according to the study, is begging "Please love me!" The financial services industry is replying, "Let me see if that is profitable first." If you are going to be serious about your brand being customer-focused, you had better take a long, hard look at the gap between what your customers are asking of you and what you are actually providing them. Remember, a brand is what the customer thinks it is, not what the company says it is.

Want to evaluate your company's Culture? Go to *Appendix B* and take a culture quiz!

A tale of two airlines

I had just boarded a Southwest Airlines flight in Orlando when I looked out the window at the Southwest Airlines jet parked beside us. In big letters printed on the side of the plane was a bold message: "Free bags fly here," with a big arrow pointing downward to the cargo compartment door. Southwest does not charge bag fees unless you're checking more than two bags. With the customer-*unfriendly* trend being that many airlines now charge fees for checked baggage, Southwest Airlines has chosen to use its aircraft as billboards to bring attention to its customer-*friendly* practices.

Southwest Airlines also aggressively promotes its generous and easy-to-use mileage rewards program. Many of us have experienced the inconvenience of trying to book a trip with a major carrier using rewards miles. It can be a real hassle navigating blackout restrictions and other excessively bureaucratic obstacles during the booking process. Once again, Southwest Airlines took something that people dislike about the competition and differentiated its own brand by launching its "Red Tape Rescue" television ads. One of the ads shows a hapless family at the airport being wrapped up in red tape by three guys from a competitor's airline. Along come the good guys from Southwest who cut through the red tape and set the family free. The message is, "No red tape at Southwest when you use your rewards points to book flights."

Southwest Airlines does a great job of taking issues that upset travelers and turning them into positive brand culture statements. The carrier plays the role of the good guy, competitors are the bad guys. When I mention the name Southwest Airlines to other air travelers, the response I most often hear is, "I love Southwest."

How does Southwest do it?

During the golden age of air travel, the 1950's and 1960's, airlines promoted hotel-quality customer service. I remember when taking a flight was a big event, for which passengers would don their Sunday best attire. They expected a "high-end" experience where they would even be served full meals on most flights.

How different it is today! Air travel has become a commodity, not much different than boarding a bus. But Southwest sees it differently. The airline excels in service quality and efficiency.

Service quality. Southwest takes pride in treating its customers well. The airline is widely known for the good-natured attitudes of its employees. Having fun is part of their Culture.[7] Humor is often used in public address announcements, both at the gates and on board flights. I recall such an announcement on a completely uneventful flight to Las Vegas. Right after the plane touched down, the flight attendant turned on his microphone, took a long deep breath, and announced to the passengers, "Whew...we made it!" The passengers erupted in laughter.

Posters in the gate area support the good-natured spirit, featuring cheerful employees taking delight in helping customers. Leaving San Antonio recently, I saw a large poster-portrait of just a smiling ramp worker saying, "We love your bags. So they fly free."

On board, the Southwest crew is pleasant but the frills are few. After all, you booked on a discount airline, remember? Your seat is fairly comfortable and you will very likely be on time. Somehow, it all works just fine, as expected. Something else contributes to your sense of satisfaction: The plane. The Southwest fleet is made up of one type of aircraft, the Boeing 737.[8] It is an integral part of the Southwest brand. Because of the consistency of the fleet, customers know exactly what to expect every time they fly on Southwest. Fly on Delta, Continental, or United and you could wind up on one of several different types of aircraft from small regional planes to jumbo jets, all with different headroom, leg room, noise levels, and overhead bins. Southwest delivers consistency on every flight, just like Darden does at each and every restaurant.

I usually fly out of Albany, New York, these days, and Southwest Airlines is my first choice. I will take a happy crew on a Southwest 737 any day in lieu of flying on a competitor's less comfortable regional jet.

Efficiency. To operate a profitable discount airline, costs need to be under control. One way Southwest achieves this is by flying, again, one type of aircraft. It currently operates approximately 550 Boeing 737 jets which fly an average of six flights per day. This aircraft model is a proven workhorse and a reliable, efficient machine. Although it has been around for a while, modifications to the original 737 design continue to improve the plane. Cabin extensions have increased capacity and passenger comfort. Winglets, which are small extensions to the wing tips, have reduced fuel consumption along with new, more advanced engines.

Flying only one type of plane yields other benefits. Maintenance, repairs, and parts are more efficiently managed. Flight and ground-crew training is easier. This is dramatically illustrated in a case study of Southwest conducted by Dartmouth's Tuck School of Business.[9] It included this example of efficiency on the ground.

"From the time a plane landed until it was ready for takeoff took approximately 20 minutes at Southwest, and required a ground crew of four plus two people at the gate. By comparison, turnaround time at United Airlines was closer to 35 minutes and required a ground crew of 12 plus three gate agents."

Fast ground turnaround is an important part of the Southwest strategy. Planes don't make money on the ground!

Southwest has also mastered the subtle art of knowing how to charge a fee and make customers feel good about it. For example: Southwest charges a fee if you want "early bird" check-in for your flight. And guess what? Passengers love it! Why do they love this, yet they don't love it when airlines charge to check luggage? The answer is choice. You don't have to pay for the early check-in, but it is there as a convenience, if you want it. In contrast, you have to take luggage on a vacation and being forced to pay extra for it is annoying. In fact, some airlines now charge for carry-on bags! Personally, I find this potential revenue-generator particularly offensive. After all, by carrying my own small bag on board, I reduce the ground crew's work load, lowering the airline's costs. Throwing a fee on top of that is double-dipping at my expense. Another "great" marketing strategy!

These days, it has become increasingly difficult for most big airlines to make money. Yet, Southwest continues to buck this trend. "Year end results for 2011 marked Southwest's 39th consecutive year of profitability," according to the company's online fact sheet.[10] So, while other airlines struggle to drive income by adding fees, Southwest showcases its lack of surcharges as a means of attracting customers. Clever!

Like Walmart, Southwest is in command of the cost side of its balance sheet and therefore able to deliver better prices. Like Disney, it cultivates happy customers as a way to drive repeat business and therefore sales volume. The Southwest Airlines brand may be the best example of a brand based on both value and service.

In comparison, let's take a look at the Culture of a competitor, Delta Air Lines.

1) When Delta needed to improve income, it turned to its customers and introduced fees to check luggage. The challenge Delta has to manage with this strategy is that although it may generate needed income, it creates a risk in maintaining customer satisfaction. Customer perception of fees is generally negative.

   As a way to mitigate complaints and force loyalty, Delta then promoted its idea of a "Good Guy" strategy. Delta would waive your bag fee if you were to use its Delta Sky Miles American Express credit card. However, the card has some potentially negative terms. The one I was recently offered had an annual fee of $95 and a rate of 14. 9%, compared to my credit union card with no annual fee and a rate of 9%. Although Delta offers travelers a way to mitigate its bag check fee, it comes at a price and requires customers to change their payment behavior in order to get the offer. In addition, some travelers may not be able to qualify for the card

2) As we have previously stated, every strategy should strive to make money. Keep in mind, though, it is important that the message communicated to customers should be consistent with a company's pricing strategy. A recent Delta television commer-

cial emphasizes a philosophy of watching out for the customer. It has pictures of a Boeing 747 and an attractive flight crew. The narrator is explaining how great it is to know that in an age of inconvenience, such as restrictions at the security check, there's still an airline that has the passenger's back. This commercial's message is inconsistent with a situation that occurred in 2010 in Albany, New York, where the Port Authority had to pressure Delta to modify its pricing in the best interest of passengers.

According to the U. S Department of Transportation[11] in August of 2010, Albany airport was unfavorably known for having the highest air fares in the state of New York. It seems that one of the culprits was Delta. The airline was serving Albany with smaller, regional jets that were often sold out. This resulted in higher fares because of the aircrafts' limited capacity. On August 2, 2010, a story in the Albany Times Union stated, "Officials at the Albany County Airport Authority said they met in recent weeks with Delta Air Lines, which provides nonstop service to Atlanta. 'We expressed concern about the high fares out of Albany,' said airport spokesman Doug Myers. Delta said it will add a larger aircraft – an Airbus A319 – in the autumn. Additional capacity often can lead to reduced airfares, all else being equal."

As a result, my last flight to Tallahassee, Florida, out of Albany, which in the past cost approximately $550 round trip, was now only $300. The first leg, to Atlanta, was on an Airbus A319 with 138 seats instead of what had previously been on a small regional jet. The final leg, to Tallahassee, was now on an MD 80, which also seats 138 passengers, instead of what had typically been just a regional jet or turboprop. In both cases the planes were full, validating just how much demand existed on those routes. This improvement begs the question, "Why didn't Delta use larger planes sooner?"Assuming that Delta is concerned about its customers, the negative publicity generated by the Port Authority about Delta's fares sent the opposite message.

3) If charging a fee is a source of customer dissatisfaction, waiving that fee can have the opposite effect. Here is an example of how Delta missed such an opportunity by placing profit ahead of

customer satisfaction, resulting in negative brand perception.

My daughter, Tansy, had booked a flight on Delta through Priceline. com from Jacksonville to Los Angeles. Two days before her cross-country trip, she broke her foot and ended up in a cast. The orthopedic surgeon, as expected, told her she would not be going to LA. Five hours on a plane without the ability to elevate her foot would not favor healing. When I called Priceline to inquire about rescheduling the flight, the agent apologized for my daughter's misfortune and asked me if she was hospitalized. I stated no, she was on crutches with a purple foot and under doctor's orders to not travel. He said, "I am so sorry, sir, you must pay Delta's $150 change fee because she is not in the hospital."

He suggested that if I were to call Delta directly, they would help. So I called Delta, but the Delta agent directed me back to Priceline. Nothing like being caught in the middle! An opportunity to build loyalty through service recovery was lost by both companies.

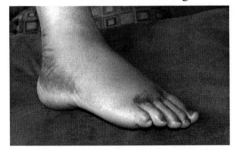

Tansy's swollen and broken foot.

Delta's promise to watch the passenger's back, was inconsistent with my experience. Tansy was under a doctor's orders to not fly, but Delta left me with an impression that it didn't care. In comparison, Southwest's standard policy is fee-free flight changes.

This experience highlights my earlier comment, "Your brand is not what *YOU* think it is. It's what your *CUSTOMERS* think it is." Delta spends a fortune telling me things I could care less about. I don't feel good about paying baggage fees. I do not want to pay a high rate and annual fee for a credit card when my credit union card has a better rate and no fees. And if I have to change my flight, especially in an emergency, a $150 change fee really tests my loyalty! Delta is touting a brand promise that is inconsistent with the customer experience it has provided me.

On the other hand, Southwest Airlines tells me I won't pay to check my bags or to change flights, that their employees care about me, and the planes are comfortable. And every time I fly South-

SOLVING THE BRAND PUZZLE

west, that's exactly the way it is.

So how does the public, in general, feel about these two airlines? Airline customer satisfaction is measured by the American Customer Satisfaction Index[12], a respected, privately-funded economic indicator that polls post-purchase consumer sentiment. In 2012 airlines, as a category, scored 67 on a scale of 1 – 100. Southwest scored 77 compared to Delta's score of 67.

CULTURE

Elements of Culture
Philosophy
Products
Services
Behaviors
Actions
Skills
Consistency
Assessment
Measurement

Let your customer tell you how you're doing

It's nice to know when your organization, its products, level of service, and employees are performing well. But it's even better to know when they are not! Then you can make corrections and fill voids. You should strive to be nothing less than best-in-class for whatever business you are in.

How can you know how your service quality is perceived unless you ask your customers? You can't. Customer feedback is an essential tactic for maintaining brand integrity. You should regularly conduct customer surveys to assess and measure how well you are doing.

During your last visit to Disney's Magic Kingdom, you probably didn't realize you were a potential survey candidate from the moment you walked through the gate. Disney begins its survey process at the entrance and continues with surveys throughout the park until you leave. The entrance surveys are short and sweet, where you might be asked something simple like, "What is your zip code?" As you progress through the park, surveys become longer, with exit interviews being the most comprehensive - probing impressions about your experiences within the park. If you are chosen for a more extensive satisfaction survey after your trip, you will likely get it about six weeks after your visit. The six week time frame assures Disney that you have first received your credit card statement. Why is this important? Because your true opinion of value will be more accurate after you have received your bill!

In the research industry, there are several research methods used to measure customer satisfaction. They include live interview, phone, mail, and internet. I recommend using a research specialist to survey your customers because customer research is a tricky business and you will want the most accurate results. Allow your researcher to use a consistent strategy in order to build the most accurate reference points and benchmarks. Make sure you target enough customers for an accurate measure, and conduct your surveys frequently in order to keep your pulse on all parts of your organization.

Careful consideration should be given to the development of survey questions. The questions should provide specific answers that can be acted upon to improve customer satisfaction and brand perception in the future.

Surveys should measure the specific topics that influence the overall satisfaction score. Only by isolating problems can tactics then be targeted to improve each area.

On past occasions, I have hired Bancography Inc., a financial-services consulting firm based in Birmingham, Alabama, to conduct customer satisfaction surveys. Their format is useful in the way it compiles actionable results. For example, in my surveys they ask 14 questions. Five questions evaluate overall opinions about the company. Nine questions focus on the point of contact experience. From the compiled answers, we are able to see which questions are affecting results and develop action plans accordingly. For example, one question that was adversely impacting the scores asked, "Were you offered other products?"

We call this the cross-sell question. The results were quite low, prompting management action to improve product training and customer interviewing skills.

Results should "drill down" to isolate accountability. In my Bancography example, we were also able to divide results by region, office, department, and employee. This level of detail was extremely useful in isolating issues, allowing us to focus on those managers and specific employees needing attention. This level of detail connects the customer to the performance appraisal and scorecard, greatly improving accountability.

Through advances in technology, automation has simplified the survey process for every industry. For example, several research companies enable businesses to program data processing systems to periodically generate customer lists and trigger surveys. The results are then automatically made available to management via the internet. This is an effective way to assure accurate, ongoing measurement and reporting with a minimal amount of work.

Technology also enables companies to invite customers to participate in on-line surveys and reward them with coupons or prize giveaways. Darden, for example, offers every guest a survey invitation. It is printed on every receipt. Just go online, answer a few questions, and you could win a prize. This is how Darden keeps its finger on the pulses of its guests at 1,900 restaurants.

Bon appétit!

The next time you visit Red Lobster, I recommend the fresh Atlantic salmon cooked on the wood-fire grill. With restaurant managers like Bob, who are willing to make a fish run, you'll enjoy the freshest salmon available.

CHAPTER 5

Sensory Experience
The Olfactory Factor: Fishy Fish and Fragrant Flowers

Our local grocery store is only a few years old and makes a good first impression from the outside. It's an attractive building with a nicely landscaped parking lot and entrance area.

Inside, the bakery, floral, deli, and produce departments are grouped in close proximity to one other. In these departments one finds many of the products touted as "fresh" by the store's advertising. It's here that shoppers' olfactory senses kick into high gear, taking in the rich aromas all around.

The seafood department is also located in this area, just beyond the produce and bakery departments. Shellfish, clams, and mussels are displayed on ice tables in the aisles, adjacent to the fresh greens cooler and the fresh-baked goods kiosks.

Sometimes, when KC and I enter this supermarket, we are taken aback by a strong, unpleasant odor – the appetite-damping stench of seafood past its prime. Unfortunately, this grim whiff of fish, which should not smell at all when fresh, overwhelms all the other delightful scents – the aroma of freshly baked bread, the perfume of fresh flowers, and the bright burst of citrus and pineapple from the produce department. Although this is a newer store, well stocked and nicely merchandised, the Sensory Experience is deeply flawed by the pungent odor of old shellfish wafting from the ice displays at the back of the store. A negative brand impression is formed. How does one know if everything else is genuinely fresh, when the store appears to be selling seafood on the cusp of being rotten?

Brand identity is a total Sensory Experience. We tend to think of visual elements first, initially associating a brand with graphic design elements like a logo, sign, or the distinctive architecture of a familiar storefront. But we actually use all our senses, including the sense of smell, when forming an impression of a company's brand.

Here is an example of how Disney, an acknowledged master of brand marketing, skillfully leverages an aroma to underscore the freshness of its products, and subsequently builds confidence in everything it sells. On your next visit to the Magic Kingdom in Orlando, Florida, walk down the right side of "Main Street USA," looking toward Cinderella's Castle. About halfway through the setting, you will amble alongside the bakery. That part of your walk will be dominated by the aroma of fresh baking bread. While standing in front of the bakery, look up and you will see a vent in the soffit above your head. Although the ovens are at the back of the bakery, Disney "pumps" the baking bread aroma through the vent and out to the sidewalk to entice passersby. Even if you resist the temptation of the bakery, your hunger-triggering Sensory Experience may soon have you searching for a restaurant. Conversely, back at our supermarket in New York, you may instead be searching for the door!

Doing it right

If you live in certain areas of the northeast, you may have visited a Wegman's market. Unlike our present local grocery store, only appropriate aromas are prevalent at Wegman's.

Entering this delightful food store is a bit like walking into Disney's Magic Kingdom. Every department is superlative. Wegman's brilliantly communicates a brand, and therefore a company, that is apparently determined to be the best in the world by re-inventing the supermarket.

At Wegman's, the meat, deli, seafood, and bakery departments

fancifully recast the best elements of an old-world, outdoor food market. Every department is the best it can be, featuring imported delicacies, exotic cheeses, health foods, and gleaming produce. The store even has a restaurant that feels like a European sidewalk café, displaying a tempting array of freshly prepared options from sushi to pizza. The atmosphere achieves a total Sensory Experience, establishing the store as a multipurpose destination.

When we lived near Philadelphia, my family and I loved to shop at Wegman's in Downingtown, Pennsylvania. We often planned our grocery shopping forays for lunchtime arrival so we could enjoy the cafe. It was such a pleasure to shop at Wegman's that I can't even tell you how the prices compared with its competitors. Price alone simply didn't matter. As much as we love where we live today, we truly miss having Wegman's close to home!

The impact of multi-sensory perception

Sight, sound, smell, touch, and taste all strongly impact a customer's brand perception. Think about your impressions as you use a product or visit an establishment. You may be surprised at how all of your senses form your opinions. Consider sound, for example.

I recall the first time I flew to the Bahamas. As I boarded the aircraft, instrumental Latin rhythms played over the plane's speaker system. Mostly due to the music, I felt my vacation had begun even before the plane left the gate. Thus, sound played an important role in forming my impression of the airline.

Have you ever watched a parade at the Walt Disney World Magic Kingdom? Why is the sound so rich no matter where you stand along the parade route? The answer is that not only is the superior sound system discretely tucked into the landscaping, but the sound track actually follows the parade. Audio synchronization, triggered at frequent intervals by sensors installed in the pavement, cues the music to the passing floats.

If you are a car enthusiast and enjoy the purr of the V8 engine in your Mustang, chances are the exhaust pipes were carefully tuned in a sound laboratory. Engine sound isn't some ancillary afterthought to auto makers. When it comes to cars, these details are important. In fact, the multi-sensory perception of a new car is formed by the sound of the engine and entertainment system, the proverbial new car smell, the feel of the leather or cloth seat covers, and the obvious importance of visual appeal. These elements all combine to build a carefully crafted emotional impression of the product. The industry as a whole endeavors to optimize the buyer experience at every possible opportunity, including fine-tuning the engine's exhaust sound. Maybe this is one reason why autos are among the highest rated purchase categories in the annual American Customer Satisfaction Index[1] survey.

Touch can influence one's sensory impression of a brand. For example, the last time you bought a piece of upholstered furniture, how heavily did the feel of the fabric influence your purchase decision? I once purchased a couch without involving my wife in the process. Big mistake! We ended up selling it on Craig's List because she couldn't stand the unnatural texture of the microfiber, faux suede fabric. Durable? Perhaps. But not desirable to KC.

Here is another example of how the tactile sense affects certain purchasing decisions. Just think of the first thing you do after spying a garment you like on a clothing rack. As you carefully touch the fabric your Sensory Experience influences your opinion of value, comfort, and quality of the potential wardrobe addition.

Taste is just as critical as all the other senses. Have you ever returned to a restaurant because the food tasted bad? Of course not! Taste trumps all – far surpassing nutrition – in the food industry. Many Americans are becoming obese because they are addicted to especially delectable foods and beverages, many of which contain excessive calorie counts. Furthermore, artificial flavorings have become a multi-billion dollar industry[2] with many professional kitchens using these additives to enhance taste in a way that is hard to match at home. Why? Because the success of their food product or restaurant depends almost wholly on taste.

How do you feel when you visit the restroom at a restaurant? Does the thought, "clean restroom, clean kitchen" come to mind? When you are getting ready to eat, the appearance and smell of a restroom may affect your appetite, especially if it is dirty and stinks! In the men's room at a particularly bad highway truck stop, I recall once seeing this line of memorable graffiti, "Flush twice, it's a long way to the kitchen." Ouch... not a very good testimonial for a Sensory Experience at a restaurant.

One restaurant that makes a particularly positive restroom impression is our favorite diner in Saugerties, New York, the Starway Café. The first time my wife visited the ladies' room in this establishment, she was so surprised by its sparkling cleanliness, she actually complimented the hostess on its sanitary impressiveness. The Starway Café has good food, and the staff treats us very well. But our brand impression was first formed in the restroom. Imagine that! Clean restroom, clean kitchen. These details seriously matter.

Visual identity is typically the anchor of a brand impression in the consumer's mind. Drive past a mall and critique the stores for visual identity. Here are some dominant impressions you are likely to experience:

- Target – notice the Bull's eye logo and the color red.
- Home Depot – the logo type and the color orange suggest the stenciled signs often seen around construction sites.
- Best Buy – the store façade is dominated by a big yellow and blue price tag.

In all of these examples, the visual imagery triggers a specific memory impression. If you are looking for a soft drink, and you prefer the predictable quality of Coca-Cola, the familiar red-and-white script logo, not its actual taste, guides you to your beverage preference in the convenience store cooler. Taste reinforces your selection, of course, but your eyes guide the choice. So, visual elements such as logos and colors create top-of-mind brand awareness, and ultimately drive sales.

What's in a logo?

In 2012, New York-based Interbrand, the world's leading brand consultancy, ranked Coca-Cola the top global brand[3], a distinction Coca-Cola has achieved for 13 consecutive years. I would bet we can all conjure up a visual image of the Coca-Cola logo. When it comes to visual identity, a company's logo is its foremost recognized brand element.

SENSORY EXPERIENCE

Brand Manual
  Logo Standards
  Brand Definitions
  Graphics Standards
  Sign Standards
Communications
  Advertising
  Public Relations
  Internal Communications
Total Sensory Appeal

Three additional examples of memorable logos are Target, Home Depot, and Best Buy. They ranked in the top five of Interbrand's US retail brands[4]. Guess who ranked first? Walmart.

A few years ago, an Australian trademarks attorney, Nicholas Weston, conducted a survey of tattoo artists. He was seeking to discover which brands were so beloved that customers had actually paid to have the company logos inked into their skin as permanent body art. According to his first annual *Tattooed Brands Global Survey,* conducted in 2009, Harley Davidson was the most "tattooed" brand[5], followed by Nike. Artists surveyed said Coca-Cola ranked 14th. Imagine that, a soft drink! Millions of people paid out of their own pockets to promote a corporation's logo. I can perhaps relate to Harley presenting a cult brotherhood image, but a soft drink? That is amazing brand equity!

What else do you "see" in a brand?

The visual brand may begin with logo recognition, but several other aesthetic elements reinforce the brand and the impression formed about that brand. Store design, signage graphics and placement, and color play a key brand-building role. Think about the multitude of visual impressions communicated by the typical modern retail store, as a series of overlapping, reinforcing experiences which build brand perception in this way:

Advertisement. Companies with strong brand equity commu-

Brand Manual
  Logo Standards
  Brand Definitions
  Graphics Standards
  Sign Standards
Communications
  Advertising
  Public Relations
  Internal Communications
Total Sensory Appeal

nicate in a consistent way. If a catchy television commercial, or a clever print ad, captures your attention, color and visual identity will make the brand association. If you see a hot product at a great price, you might say to a friend, "There's a sale on cameras at Best Buy." If the ad were not so brand-relevant, you might instead ask, "Now where did I see that camera sale?"

Sign. In response to a Best Buy ad, an interested customer will drive to the shopping center. Bold, clearly-identifiable signage at the roadside entrance will reassure the customer they have arrived at the Best Buy store.

Storefront. Once in the parking lot, especially at a large shopping center, the storefront is the next brand recognition element. If it is easy to spot, the customer is wholly reassured – destination found! Best Buy's exterior design is easy to spot and brand-consistent across its franchise of 1,100 US stores.

Interior design. The customer's visual journey continues inside the Best Buy store. A greeter is available at the entrance, the layout is easy to navigate, and there is ample signage and staff to guide and serve. Lastly, the store motif reflects the high-tech feeling of its core business of consumer electronics.

Staff attire. Employees are the human brand channel and their appearance is an important part of the store's visual identity. Best Buy associates are clearly identifiable by their company-branded royal blue polo shirts and khaki slacks. When customers need them, they are easy to find.

Point of sale. At last! The customer arrives at the camera department. The advertised product is highlighted with a "Sale" or "As Advertised" notation and the product information presents features and benefits with clear descriptions.

The visual trail that began with the original ad is now complete. At every critical step, visual identity succeeded in capturing the customer's attention, guiding the way, and satisfying the reason for the journey.

Seeing is believing, and so are hearing, smelling, touching and tasting!

Every time your company name, products, staff, store, website, or advertisement makes contact with a customer, a brand impression is formed. The multi-Sensory Experience plays a dominant role in how that impression is formed.

It is important to always remember that every facet of your business evokes a sensory response and plays a role in how your brand is perceived. Consider once again: Your brand is not what you say it is, but what your customer thinks it is.

CHAPTER 6

The Digital Brand

My dear wife, KC, recently bought a pair of eye glasses online, which is noteworthy because she doesn't like to shop on the internet. Not only that, but the glasses cost $1,000, and she loves them! Now, of all the things to buy online, prescription eye glasses? What you should also know about KC is that she has little tolerance for poorly communicated information. For KC, it has to be concise and straightforward.

KC spends her day in front of a computer. With age, it has become increasingly difficult for her to find glasses that are comfortable when changing focus from the computer screen to printed documents on her desk. She tried to manage this issue with bifocals and multiple pairs of prescription glasses. Yet, she was still dealing with eyestrain and headaches.

One day, she saw an ad on CNN for Superfocus glasses. Testimonials from celebrities, including magician Penn Jillette and actor Joel Grey, extolled the virtues of Superfocus prescription eye wear. When she visited the Superfocus website, she quickly found more video testimonials, one of which was by a customer who described KC's work environment exactly and said Superfocus technology provided the perfect solution for him. KC also watched a video demonstration on the website that explained how the glasses work, utilizing a unique adjustable-focus technology. And just when she was becoming drawn to the product, she went to the prices and… gulp… a steep thousand bucks! She asked me what I thought, and I invoked the secret-to-36-years-of-marriage rule, "Whatever makes you happy, darling!"

KC decided to go for it because an improvement in her eyesight, which would also eliminate her headaches, was worth a grand. Although Superfocus has a network of eye doctors who offer the product, none were close by. The comprehensive website, however, made KC confident enough to place an online order, complete with a 30-day, full refund, satisfaction guaranteed promise. She received her glasses, custom-made to her prescription, in about three weeks. To this day, she frequently comments on how much less eye strain she feels when she puts them on for computer work.

Why is KC's e-commerce experience noteworthy and relevant to *Solving the Brand Puzzle*? The answer is this: Two of the four puzzle pieces, Sensory Experience and Culture, are difficult to communicate via the internet. Yet Superfocus pulled it off.

Let's take a closer look at the unique challenges of selling products via e-commerce.

Sensory Experience. Only two of the five senses can realistically be used for online communication: Sight and sound. In the electronic world, smell, taste, and touch are no longer *real*, but rather *virtual*, requiring us to imagine the fragrance of the perfume, taste of the sauce, or feel of the fabric. Therefore, it is the skill of the photographer, copy writer, and website designer that influences our buying decisions in the e-commerce world.

Culture. In the real world, culture is communicated by face-to-face interaction with customers. E-commerce, on the other hand, eliminates that human interaction. On the internet, culture is communicated remotely by technology. As a result, it is the responsibility of automated processes, not people, to elicit an emotional reaction from the customer.

Superfocus managed these two puzzle pieces with great success. In analyzing KC's sales experience, we find that Superfocus clearly satisfied all of her needs. Let's look more deeply at how they achieved this.

The Superfocus Sensory Experience

Sight. Visually, the Superfocus website is outstanding. It presents bold close-ups of people fashionably modeling the glasses, and crisp technical illustrations that explain how the glasses work.

Sound. Videos of customer testimonials are professionally done and quite convincing. The Superfocus testimonials do an excellent job of selling the product.

Touch. Although you can't actually touch the glasses online, the website helps the visitor imagine how it would feel to wear them. For anyone who has worn bifocals, testimonials and photos comparing them to Superfocus glasses clearly demonstrate the difference. Also, a close-up illustration of the sliding adjustment on the bridge helps the viewer imagine how easy the glasses would be to operate.

The Superfocus Culture

Friendly. The website was simple, easy to navigate, and informative. The entire story about the product is told in five parts, each with its own button, without scrolling.

Trustworthy. Integrity was established within a few minutes. Superfocus presented a NASA endorsement, a Wall Street Journal Innovation Award, and access to several customer testimonials, all on a cleanly-designed home page.

Value. The sales experience overcame "sticker shock" with an effective presentation of a unique and effective solution for KC's vision challenges. The message communicated by the demonstrative home page was clear: "They're worth it."

Risk-free. The sales process mitigated any fear of the purchase with a no-risk, 30-day guarantee. The guarantee popped up on the home page when I hovered over the link, making it practically unavoidable.

Helpful. The ordering process was easy, and customer friendly. Follow-up service was excellent. When Superfocus received KC's prescription, there was an important piece of information missing: The measurement of distance between her pupils. A very friendly, competent Superfocus employee called KC and quickly resolved the matter. So, in addition to its very effective website, Superfocus took advantage of a telephone-based customer service opportunity to enhance the online sales experience.

At every touch point, Superfocus effectively eliminated obstacles and delivered satisfaction. For the effort in creating a well-designed cyber experience, they now have a satisfied, hard-to-sell customer touting their product.

Doing it right

One of the most well-known and popular online stores is Amazon.com. Founded in 1994 by Jeff Bezos, its website launched in 1995, and the company has since become the world's largest online retailer, attracting over 600,000,000 visitors annually.[1] Amazon has been a bellwether for consumer internet commerce ever since. Amazon.com was heavily critiqued and closely scrutinized in its early days. In the midst of the dot-com to dot-gone bubble of the mid-90s, the company managed to survive. While the world watched many internet companies come and go, questioning whether the public would ever fully embrace the internet as a retail shopping source, Amazon struggled to achieve profitability but ultimately won. It's now the world's largest online retailer. How wrong the doubters were!

Amazon.com was originally known only as an online bookstore. Traditional bookstores had always been esteemed as sacred places, yet Amazon challenged the paradigm by introducing e-commerce to book selling. Today, Amazon.com offers dependably low prices on just about anything a consumer might need: Books, movies, music, electronics, auto parts, food… you name it! The company's vision statement says it all:

> Our vision is to be earth's most customer centric company; to build a place where people can come to find and discover anything they might want to buy online.

Amazon lives up to the promise of finding anything by supplementing its own inventory with a network of affiliated businesses whose products and e-commerce are integrated into the Amazon. com web site.

For my daughter, Kestrel, and her husband, Alex, Amazon.com is the new Walmart. They buy almost everything from Amazon, including dog food, specialty foods, kitchen appliances, utensils, tools, health and beauty aids, vitamins, games, clothing, and, of course, books. Amazon offers free, two-day shipping with its Amazon Prime Service, a choice that Kestrel and Alex opted to get. Amazon even offers auto-shipment for some of their regular purchases. Kestrel informed us recently that she is also not renewing her Sam's Club membership because they no longer use it, thanks to Amazon.

Staying true to its roots, Amazon continues to be a dominant book seller. The company has asserted competitive pressure on the entire book retailing industry. For example, in 2011 Borders bookstore threw in the towel; the corporation filed for bankruptcy, and liquidated the chain. The bookstore chain had been "battered by competition from internet retailers and burdened with too much debt," according to the Wall Street Journal.[2]

Not only has Amazon revolutionized how we buy books, it has revolutionized how we read them. Its Kindle book reader is a huge hit, touted as "the most popular e-reader in the world." With its built-in wireless connectivity, Kindle users can download books directly to the device from anywhere a cell phone connection exists. The Kindle also enables a user to store a library of favorite books and share them with other users.

Amazon's leaders apparently also recognized they could make a tidy profit by directly publishing and distributing books. By creating a mainstream venue for authors to publish themselves, the company enabled authors to bypass the cumbersome traditional publishing industry and publish their own books as e-books. This also created more demand for the Kindle. Today, authors can even publish hard copies through Amazon and make them available on demand. A major investment in the traditional, large print run is no longer required. By creating a new supply chain for its retail sales and its popular e-reader, Amazon has "re-written the book" on how we buy, read, and publish books.

In the context of *Solving the Brand Puzzle*, Amazon has designed a customer experience that is noteworthy. The Amazon.com website is:

Consistent. Product searches dependably result in broad selections and great prices.

Convenient. Amazon account holders, who are looking to purchase a particular item, can use the one-click, express checkout and have their entire search, purchase, and shipping experience completed in less than two minutes. I know this because I have done it…more than once. To further enhance customer convenience, Amazon frequently offers shoppers free standard shipping with a minimum order of $25.

Helpful. Amazon has no pushy clerks. In a live retail checkout, I am annoyed if a clerk tries to cross-sell me something. It is almost like a duel: The clerk is trying to manipulate me, so I am inclined to resist. Ironically, however, Amazon's website cross-sells constantly, and I view it is a convenience. I love the line they use, "People who purchased this book also purchased these," and the website displays images of several suggestions. Amazon offers me a Carole King album as I shop for James Taylor, and I appreciate the gesture because I like both artists. At Amazon.com, cross-selling becomes a courtesy. By associating products intuitively, and not "pushing" products for the sake of achieving an additional sale, the website creates a more intimate experience. Amazon excels by linking its well developed e-commerce technology to its massive inventory.

So does it really work for Amazon? Here are the numbers. Amazon went public on May 15, 1997 with an initial stock offering of $18 per share. On August 30, 2011, Amazon stock was trading at $210.92[3] per share. There had been three splits along the way, transforming the original share into 12 shares with a combined value of $2,531.04. Now that's a digital brand!

Making hard-to-find stuff easy to find

Thanks to the internet, smaller businesses offering specialized goods and services can reach enormous markets. No longer are these businesses dependent on local traffic. The internet can bring customers to them.

Within ten miles of my home, there are four big-box home improvement stores, and two local hardware stores. You would think I could find a part for my John Deere lawnmower at one of them, but I couldn't. My mower was purchased at Lowe's, yet I found that Lowes is not where you find a specialized small replacement part. I went online and discovered that the nearest John Deere dealer was 20 miles away. When I called them, they also did not have the part, but offered to order one and have it in a week, at which point I could go pick it up. OK, back to Google.

I found myself visiting the website of a store 1,000 miles away in Watseka, Illinois, called GreenPartStore.com. I was soon looking at a detailed, illustrated parts catalog of my mower. Sure enough, I easily found my part. After completing an easy checkout process, I was pleased to see that delivery would be in four days, right to my front door. A 40-mile road trip to my "local" dealer would not be necessary. The entire experience took less than an hour, saved time and gasoline, and left me very satisfied. A company in Watseka, Illinois had found a customer in Saugerties, New York, thanks to the internet.

Let's take a closer look at the GreenPartStore.com digital brand from the *Solving the Brand Puzzle* perspective. The "About Us" link on the website identifies the company as a subsidiary of a John Deere dealership with seven full-time employees. Two of the job descriptions contain interesting responsibilities. One is the webmaster; the other is the eBay administrator. From this page of the website, I drew two conclusions: The company is small, but it is committed to e-commerce.

GreenPartStore.com's parent company, Arends Hogan Walker LLC has been a John Deere dealer since 1932. Although I never sat in on any of their strategic planning sessions, the company's decision to embrace the internet may have involved a hypothetical scenario such as this one: The owners, like all business owners, wanted to make more money. They recognized a huge opportunity (remember TWSO?) and established a strategy for taking advantage of it. They realized that, via the internet, they could dramatically boost sales by expanding their market beyond the local market in Watseka. To do so, however, would require fast, reliable fulfillment and delivery of orders. This meant they would need to expand their parts inventory to minimize backorders. Fortunately, the higher cost of increasing the parts inventory would be offset by the expected increase in sales volume.

The reason this strategy would have been sound is because John Deere does not sell parts directly to the public. Instead, the company refers all sales to its dealer network. Given the scope of the John Deere parts catalog, it is unlikely that most local dealers could stock a large enough inventory to prevent walk-in customers from having to wait for parts. Arends Hogan Walker probably recognized that by expanding its parts inventory, it would provide the level of service it sought, become a successful internet company, and achieve its desired increase in sales. GreenPartStore.com was born.

Here is how, in my observation, GreenPartStore.com put the puzzle pieces of its brand together:

Strategic Vision. Increase sales volume with internet sales.

Management. Provide exceptional service by expanding the parts inventory and deploying a friendly and easy-to-use e-commerce experience. Control costs with a small but efficient staff. Optimize website search performance so the digital storefront is easy to find.

Culture. Create a website image that is wholesome and farm-friendly in keeping with John Deere, a credible brand with deep roots in agriculture. Show photos of their down-to-earth employees with whom customers would want to do business, even if they couldn't meet them personally.

Sensory Experience. Use the trademark John Deere colors of green and yellow because they are such a widely recognized brand visual element. This will immediately create a connection between GreenPartStore.com and John Deere while communicating a sense of brand spirit.

My conclusion is that small businesses *can* thrive when they put all the brand puzzle pieces together. GreenPartStore.com has successfully differentiated itself from Lowes and Home Depot on the internet the same way Montano's did on Main Street when it figured out how to compete with Walmart and national shoe chain stores.

Impact of the internet on traditional business

The internet has influenced, for better and worse, traditional business categories. Many businesses that are dependent on walk-in traffic have embraced the internet and changed their business practices. Others have seen online automation eliminate the need for storefronts altogether. Here are some examples:

Restaurants. Dining is a live experience. Since no one has yet figured out how to dine online, the restaurant customer experience will still be "real." However, the internet has changed the business in other ways. Restaurants can build a virtual storefront to romance menus and vividly describe the tastes they offer. They can create an online following, using email and social media, to transmit special menu items and discount incentives. In addition, it's easier to monitor customer satisfaction utilizing online surveys.

But with opportunity comes consequence. If customers aren't satisfied, negative online reviews can cause some serious reputational damage, resulting in a negative impact on business. Now, instead of complaints being shared with a handful of friends and relatives, they can be broadcast to thousands!

Airlines. Like dining, air travel will always be a live activity. Therefore, airlines need to continue providing an exceptional passenger experience. The internet changed the game, though, with the introduction of e-commerce.

Customers can now buy their tickets and print their boarding passes at home. Airlines can also market electronically, communicating "deals" via email. One can even plan an entire vacation, with transportation, hotels, car rental, and activities included, at a single travel or airline web site. Because of the Internet, an entire traditional category of businesses – small, local travel agencies – has declined dramatically[4].

Autos. Cars and trucks are a big investment, yet the process of purchasing them always used to be an unpleasant experience. How many times have you heard someone complain about a car dealer? I liken the purchasing experience to old-fashioned horse trading, with little trust between the dealer and the customer.

The internet has changed all of that, creating a real advantage for the car buyer. Now, consumers can go online to research the value of a trade-in, the wholesale price of a new model, and open a dialog with a dealership. Auto reviews are readily available from consumers and a wide range of enthusiast resources... all with the click of a mouse.

I recently purchased a new vehicle with the help of the internet. The process provided me with a great example of an internet customer experience. After much online research, I placed a request through the Ford website to be contacted by a local dealer. One dealer contacted me 12 hours later with an offer I could not refuse. There was no haggling because I had obtained detailed pricing in advance. By the way, my request had gone to two dealerships. The second dealer contacted me two days after I had already made the purchase. Oops!

Entertainment. When it comes to movies, books, and music, just about everything has changed because of technology and the internet.

Not long ago, theaters were challenged by the threat of movie rental stores. Mom-and-pop video rental stores sprang up across the country, but were soon overwhelmed by the brand dominance of the Blockbuster and Hollywood Video rental chains. Compounding the challenge, consumers were getting more comfortable watching movies in their homes with the availability of affordable big screen, high-definition TVs and surround sound. Along came the next generation of movie distribution: Netflix and movies-on-demand. What could be more convenient than movies delivered directly to your mailbox or right to your television? Nothing, right?

But what if an on-demand movie is not available, or a customer can't wait two days for mail delivery? Now they can check availability at Redbox.com and pick up their movie at one of Redbox's 42,000 well-branded kiosks nationwide. The kiosks are conveniently located at shopping centers, supermarkets, and pharmacies – places we all visit on a regular basis. In addition, Redbox rentals cost less than cable, and there is no monthly subscription as with Netflix. Each Redbox rental costs under two dollars.

The internet has caused another change in the entertainment business. Movies are now available online from other retailers. For example, Apple was especially smart in making movies available for instant download to a variety of devices, including its popular iPhone and iPad. As a matter of strategic vision, Apple recognized the profitable potential in becoming a content provider for the products it manufactured.

Retail. Understanding both the threat and potential of the internet, most major retailers have added e-commerce to their strategies. Big-box and specialty retailers alike – companies such as Walmart, Lowes, Sam's Club, Best Buy, Bed Bath & Beyond, and even department stores like Macy's and Kohl's – have effectively extended their brands online.

How does technology impact the customer experience online?

Defining a strong web-based brand is no different than defining any other brand. The exception is that culture is communicated through systems and a computer interface, not by a real person. Consumers generally demand an online experience that is fast, straightforward, and delivers value. The most successful e-commerce sites have defined a new standard for satisfying consumer demands by engineering emotion into their online experience. Never before have automation and function played such an important role in providing customer satisfaction.

We have come a long way from the time when we could not figure out how to set the clock on a microwave oven to now feeling comfortable with going online to shop, bank, and do research. I believe that at least part of the reason is because the gap between the left-brain thinking process of the engineers and programmers, and the right-brain thinking process of the designers and merchants, has closed dramatically. For example, the traditional method of explaining a device's setup, functions, and operations was to provide the customer with a complicated, technically-oriented manual geared to a college-level audience. Today, the process would likely skip the manual and instead provide a "quick start" guide, simplified to a fifth-grade level of understanding. That may seem like a demeaning comment, but I believe designing for such clarity is actually a courtesy to the customer. These days, we are all too busy to spend time figuring out complicated instructions, especially for products designed to provide convenience or entertainment.

Think about how much easier it is to operate your smartphone, set up a new computer, and, yes, set the clock on your microwave. It is likely that the manufacturer took the extra step to make the experience of using the product more understandable.

The last Windows computer I purchased, from Hewlett-Packard, took me just a half-hour to set up. The entire procedure was automated. The device came with quick-start instructions only, no manual. The computer walked me through a simple step-by-step process. There were only a few preferences from which to choose; everything else was automated for me. Someone at HP realized that, for the average user, anything beyond picking a password and registering the device was a needless part of the setup experience. Plus, the easier the process, the less chance there would be for a computer-intimidated user to screw it up! Fewer calls to tech support helps keep the prices down, too.

My son-in-law, Alex, a software engineer, was critical of my HP example. From the "geek" perspective, he makes a valid argument that to accomplish simplicity, computer manufacturers have to load their machines with extra software that automates (and sometimes duplicates) existing functionality. Alex's issue was that these "bloatware" programs tend to bog down machine performance. My counterpoint was that with most new computers having multi-core processors, gigabytes of extended memory, and huge hard drives, does it really matter to the average user? Aren't these computers well-enough equipped to handle a few extra processes? He was willing to agree with the "average user" rationale. However, he insisted that in his world of hard-core gaming, where computer performance is king, he would continue to strip these "unnecessary" programs from his operating system.

Similar practices, intended to improve customer convenience, have become part of the cultures of most computer brands as well as other tech product makers. As an example of just how much progress has been made, here are two personal experiences, one bad and the other good.

The first one happened two years ago when I purchased a wireless bridge so I could access the internet from our LCD television. If you thought that setting a digital clock on the microwave oven was bad, no kidding, this gadget took two hours to set up, culminating in a 45 minute call to tech support. A few weeks after we got it to work, we had a power outage which crashed the device. After the first nightmare setup experience, we never bothered to get it running again.

The second example occurred when my daughter recently came to visit and brought with her a new device to replace the one I'd been complaining about. It was the Roku 2 XS Streaming Player, which replaced both my clumsy wireless bridge and the separate streaming player attached to it. In comparison to the complicated setup experience with the bridge, we simply plugged in the Roku and turned it on. That's all it took. It worked immediately.

To achieve this level of simplification in the digital age, some design teams include a specialist who is empathetic to the customer's perspective: Someone whose job it is to improve functionality and assure a customer-friendly experience. In this new paradigm, e-commerce works because the customer experience is now an integrated part of the engineering process. Great e-commerce websites like Amazon.com, Buy.com, and others build loyalty by treating their customers well and providing an easy-to-use process.

New technology breeds a new kind of crime

With all of this new technology, however, come new challenges for privacy and security. In addition to worrying about a thief coming through the door with a gun, we must also worry about thousands of "hackers" across the globe trying to steal our identities, money, and data. These crimes range in scope from the global theft of millions of credit cards in a bold breach of a large enterprise[5], to the methodical hacking of a point-of-sale terminal for a handful of credit card numbers at the local pizza shop. The thieves then put the credit card numbers up for sale, for a few dollars each, on the internet. Other thieves purchase the cards for illegal use until they are shut off.[6] These incidents have made the headlines on a regular basis, raising consumer awareness of e-commerce security vulnerabilities.

For a brand to be complete, it must be safe and secure. Once again, in the new age of digital crime, safety and soundness must trump convenience. When customers make online purchases, take cash from an ATM, or do their banking on the internet, they expect that the transactions are secure. Yet, the typical consumer has no idea of how secure those networks and systems really are. According to the Federal Trade Commission, some nine million Americans fall prey to identity theft every year, mostly due to credit card fraud.[7]

Not only must service culture be part of a digital brand's design, so must security. Although *Solving the Brand Puzzle* is not about cyber-security, the impact of fraud on brand perception is worth emphasizing. Providing security must be a consideration in how the customer's experience is delivered by a digital brand.

In an incident that will be scrutinized for years to come, Sony Corp. found out the hard way how serious a cyber-security attack can be. In April of 2011, hackers penetrated its popular Playstation Network, an online gaming site with over 70,000,000 subscribers. The results were catastrophic. User account information was compromised, forcing the company to shut down the entire Playstation Network for several weeks[8]. Its slow and less-than-forthcoming response to the incident left customers fuming. It cost Sony over $170 million to restore service and rebuild customer confidence[9]. This well-publicized attack highlights the importance of security and customer relations as part of the Culture of a digital brand. It also shows how costly such an attack can be on a company's reputation and its bottom line.

New type of protection for the new age of crime

Advances in technology have stimulated the start and growth of the digital security industry. There are now numerous companies that specialize in the protection of identity, data, and passwords. Some offer excellent examples of easy-to-use, customer-friendly digital brands.

One of my favorites, Equifax.com, monitors my credit reports. Equifax provides me with alerts of activities that may indicate fraud, such as suspicious credit card transactions and large changes in balances. If I were to become a victim of fraud, Equifax would also provide assistance in repairing any of the damage that would have resulted from the incident.

After logging in as a subscriber on the Equifax website, a personal dashboard appears. This dashboard is divided into four distinct sections that make it easy to understand and monitor the subscriber's credit. They are: Latest Credit Score, Current Alerts, Credit Summary, and Debt Summary. The Current Alerts tool is particularly useful. It sends email notifications of credit report activity such as credit inquiries and balance changes. By providing these email alerts, Equifax communicates important information to its customers when they need to know it. Customers do not have to remember to go seek it. This is another good example of how a digital brand can use technology to deliver outstanding service.

Another of my favorites, CrashPlan.com, is a company that provides automated file backup for personal data. Not only does CrashPlan.com provide a low-cost way to back up computer files, it does so with a great website and lots of encryption.

The CrashPlan.com website reminds me of our earlier Superfocus experience. There are young, happy faces demonstrating the product's purpose, and the site has a very clean design. It presents an endorsement from the Wall Street Journal, provides simple options to fit my needs, and offers a free trial. They explain how their software encrypts files using hard-to-hack advanced encryption before the files are sent. In addition, to reinforce my already favorable impression, CrashPlan.com lists some respectable client names, including Google, Adobe, and Cisco.

Bottom line: I back up nearly 200 gigabytes of data for about 165 bucks per two-year period (backup size is actually unrestricted.) Setup took a few minutes and I haven't thought about it since. It is completely automated and sends me email notices of backup status. How simple is that?

Passwords provide another opportunity for hackers. Many online consumers use easy-to-remember passwords, such as birthdays, kids' names, and pets' names, which can be easy for thieves to obtain. They may also use the same password for multiple purposes, adding to their vulnerability. KeePass.info provides a simple way to make passwords more secure by providing random password codes and an easy, safe way to store and retrieve them from an encrypted database. On its website, KeePass.info describes its service this way:

> KeePass is a free, open source password manager, which helps you to manage your passwords in a secure way. You can put all your passwords in one database, which is locked with one master key or a key file. So you only have to remember one single master password or select the key file to unlock the whole database. The databases are encrypted using the best and most secure encryption algorithms currently known (AES and Twofish).

Unlike other digital brands we've discussed, the KeePass.info website offers little in the way of a sensory experience. However, the KeePass concept is so simple, not to mention free, that the absence of marketing glitz is easy to forgive. Once you use it, you'll be hooked and want to tell your friends about it.

In my opinion, Equifax.com, CrashPlan.com, and KeePass.info are not only innovations of the digital age, they are outstanding examples of great e-commerce experiences and technical products that are easy-to-use and affordable. In other words, they shine as complete digital brands.

The paradigm shift

The growth of online commerce has changed the traditional way of doing business. By its very nature, e-commerce demands that automated processes replace people. Online, companies must elicit the "WOW" response without human interface. This creates the need to design a customer experience that reflects the company's brand cornerstones and mission without the benefit of employees interacting with customers.

A successful e-commerce brand must optimize its automated processes to create a safe, noteworthy, and emotional customer experience. The old days of left-brained engineers and "geeks" working independently of designers and "dreamers" are over. Both need to work together in order to create a "Superfocus" experience.

CHAPTER 7

Be a Brand Critic

There are reasons why you like certain products, services, and companies, and reasons why you do not. As previously stated in *Solving the Brand Puzzle,* a brand is what you perceive it to be, NOT what you're supposed to think it is. If you do not perceive a brand as it is intended by a company, then the company needs to re-discover its brand because the brand is flawed.

Solving the Brand Puzzle has empowered you with a formula to technically critique any company and look at the strength of its brand. Instead of just passing emotional judgment, you will now have a better understanding of your reactions. Your perceptions of a brand can now be related to how well or poorly, a company puts the four puzzle pieces together. With your new knowledge, I encourage you to begin enjoying the process of being a brand critic.

Why do good brands go bad?

One thing I wonder about when I critique brands is why successful companies go into decline. For instance, I am frustrated by the fact that many of the companies studied in Jim Collins' book, *Good to Great,* are no longer the shining examples they once were. Several are gone, period. What happened? What is even more interesting to me is looking at today's brand leaders and trying to figure out which ones will be the next to lose or gain the edge. A strong brand today must be adapted to the shifting values of customers, emerging technologies, demographic evolution, and the simple threat of great ideas going stale.

Thinking about great companies, and as an example of a personal brand critique, let's look at Starbucks. Remember, as you read this, it is not just about emotion-driven opinions. It is about viewing a brand through the lens of everything you have learned in *Solving the Brand Puzzle*.

The decline of Starbucks during the management hiatus of its passionate founder Howard Schultz, from 2000 to 2008, is a case study in how a world-beater brand can still nearly tank. During this period of rapid expansion consumer and investor confidence slipped. As a result, the company stock price eventually declined.

In December, 2007, Starbucks stock was trading at around $25 per share. One year later, it was trading at $10 and, fearing the company had become a takeover target, Starbucks' board of directors brought Schultz back to right the ship.[1]

> *"The damage was slow and quiet, incremental,*
> *like a single loose thread*
> *that unravels a sweater inch by inch."*
> *--Howard Schultz, president and CEO of Starbucks,*
> *in his book* Onward

Restoring a "laser focus" on customers, Schultz completely realigned the organization to "live and breathe Starbucks" the way its 50 million customers per week do. In the process Starbucks closed about 900 shops.[2] The strategy appeared successful. In September, 2011, the stock had recovered to a price of $37.[3]

Could Starbucks' blurring of customer focus happen again? On a July, 2011 vacation, a less than stellar Starbucks experience made me apprehensive that standards could once again be slipping. On the whole, Starbucks is a brand that commands my sincere respect. Yet, after reading *Good to Great*, who would have thought that Circuit City, and several other companies profiled in the book, were on the way down? With this in mind, and multiple Starbucks experiences taunting my brand critic's imagination, I began to wonder if Starbucks had once again taken its eye off the ball.

My brand critique began one morning while visiting a Starbucks in Tallahassee, Florida. KC and I were informed that they did not serve breakfast sandwiches. Brand inconsistency! Some Starbucks serve breakfast sandwiches and others, apparently, do not. We left disappointed and without making a purchase. As we left, the stale décor of this particular Starbucks further compounded my dissatisfaction.

Ironically, I noticed that copies of *Onward*, the Starbucks book by Howard Shultz, were prominently displayed for sale. I could not help but wonder if the brand discussed in the book was different from the one that I had just perceived.

Later during the trip we stopped at another Starbucks on the way to Orlando to catch our flight back to Albany. KC wanted a breakfast sandwich with egg and cheese, no meat. We were informed that they would have to take the meat off a pre-made sandwich. Hmmm... it dawned on me that fresh is not part of the Starbucks brand culture when it comes to food. To the credit of a well-trained clerk, however, she suggested the Veggie and Monterey Jack Artisan Breakfast Sandwich, which we purchased.

When our order arrived at the drive-up window, I took my "grande" coffee from the clerk. As I placed it in the car's cup holder, the cup collapsed in my hand. Scalding hot coffee spilled on KC and me. The Starbucks's experience was becoming one of distress. One notable exception was that, once again, our well-trained associate offered multiple apologies and gave us a free coffee coupon for our next visit. From a cultural viewpoint, she exhibited great service recovery.

Sometime later, after cleaning up the mess and heading up I-95, I asked KC if she liked her sandwich.

"It's OK but I'll never order another one," was her answer.

Although the sandwich had flecks of vegetables in the egg, it certainly was not up to the standards of a modern American vegetarian. When we later pulled into a gas station, she handed me her coffee cup to throw away. It was half full. When I mentioned this to her, she said the coffee was bitter for her personal taste.

In spite of her previous declaration, several months later, in Mystic, Connecticut, KC decided to revisit the meatless breakfast sandwich challenge at Starbucks. There were no other restaurant options nearby. Once again, she was told that her only option was having the meat removed from a packaged, grab-and-go sandwich. However, the associate assured her that she would like the result since the sandwich was made fresh... yesterday.

As a brand critic, I could not help but compare Starbucks to two of its major competitors, Panera Bread and Dunkin' Donuts.

Let's look more closely at Panera Bread. The St. Louis-based company made a strategic decision to expand nationally in 1999, and today operates approximately 1,500 restaurants across 40 states and Canada. I first dined at Panera when KC and I were vacationing in Santa Monica, California back in 2006. More than pleasantly surprised, we went back another four times during the next six days, buying coffee, breakfasts, lunches, and snacks. The Panera brand was obviously working. We kept going back for more!

Panera Bread has earned top honors from the Harris Poll EquiTrend in 2011, the Zagat 2010 Fast Food Survey, and the 2009 Sandleman & Associates Quick-Track Awards of Excellence. The company also placed in the top 25 of *Business Week*'s 2010 Customer Service Champs and *Fortune Magazine*'s 2010 list of Fastest-Growing Companies.

A Panera Bread restaurant is typically larger than a Starbucks. Like Starbucks, wi-fi is available for those wanting to "gather" while perusing the internet or catching up on e-mail. The atmosphere is new-age and trendy, styled with pleasant pieces of artwork that allude to bread baking with a European touch. I find myself comfortable connecting my laptop there, getting lost in the digital world, and writing over a light roast coffee.

Unlike Starbucks, Panera sandwiches and salads are prepared fresh while you watch. A quick look at the menu reveals a list of contemporary sandwiches, as many as six kinds of soups, and several tossed-to-order salads. The sandwiches are available on a variety of breads baked on the premises. After all, you are ordering and dining, essentially, inside a fully functional artisanal bakery.

Did Panera pull a page from the Starbucks playbook and take it to the next level? In my experience, Panera made gathering more pleasant by offering a truly fresh menu with many more choices.

Now, let's look at Dunkin' Donuts. You have to hand it to

Dunkin' Donuts. When Starbucks came along, many of us thought it was the beginning of Dunkin' Donuts' demise. Not so fast. Here is a company that, 20 years ago, offered little more than both coffee and donuts on their menu. But in response to evolving customer tastes and increased competition from Starbucks, McDonalds, and Panera, Dunkin' Donuts now offers lattes, hot breakfast selections, and a lunch menu of soup and sandwiches. The coffee and donuts are still there, fresh as ever, but their largely blue-collar clientele now have more reasons to visit other than just on the way to work.

So, instead of letting change, driven by innovative competitors, lead the company down the path of failure, Dunkin' Donuts adapted to be more competitive. The company went public in July of 2011, with a stock offering of $19 per share. As of February 10, 2012, it was trading at $28, and the company is planning a significant expansion in the western United States. Good ol' Dunkin' Donuts...still a brand that prompts a lot of people to hit the brake pedal and turn the wheel when they see the sign.

I know, I know, Starbucks has a loyal brand following. But, does my experience hint at another decline as described in Mr. Schultz's earlier quote? Is the sweater beginning to unravel again? I can't be the only one who has had similarly unsatisfying Starbucks experiences. Personally, it will influence where I buy my next cup of coffee if a Starbucks and a Panera Bread are located side-by-side.

Remember the golden rule: A brand is what the customer perceives it to be, not what the company thinks it is. As I have done in this chapter, you, too, can analyze your own perceptions of other brands. When you apply the lessons learned from those experiences to your own company, you will be on the road to developing a better brand.

Want to critique your own brand? Get started with the Brand Quiz at www.thebrandbook.net.

APPENDIX A

Brand Discovery Case Study
How to Discover your Brand and
Establish Your Brand Cornerstones

Chapter two explained the roles of Brand Discovery and Brand Cornerstones in the development of Strategic Vision, but not the process of how to develop them. This Appendix demonstrates how a team of employees in one company went through the steps of Discovering its Brand and establishing Brand Cornerstones.

Case study

This is the way a financial institution, Mid-Hudson Valley Federal Credit Union, visually branded as MHV, engaged the process of discovering its unique and compelling brand.

At the time MHV started down the path of discovery, it had nearly 60,000 members and operated 11 branch offices in a three-county region. (As a matter of clarification, credit unions are cooperatives that refer to their customers as members. This is because they are not-for-profit organizations with specific eligibility requirements. Income generated by a credit union is distributed to the entire membership in the form of better rates and lower fees. Conversely, banks distribute income in the form of dividends to their shareholders.)

MHV's competitive playing field was brutal, and included large banks, community banks, and other credit unions. It's generally considered that about 1,500 to 3,000 households are required to support each branch location of a financial institution. In MHV's over-supplied market, however, there were only 750 households supporting each of its existing locations. Thinking logically, there just wasn't enough demand to sustain the number of financial institutions in the market.

Compounding the problem, the time frame of the discovery process was from 2009 - 2011, when the economy was in the grip of a recession and extended slump. This anemic economy and predatory competitive environment created the "wake up call" MHV needed to provoke change throughout the company.

Management contracted the research firm Bancography, of Birmingham, Alabama, to conduct a survey. Concerns were validated when 400 telephone survey interviews revealed inconsistent brand awareness and low brand differentiation. This meant that a number of local residents didn't know who MHV was. And, many who did failed to recognize it as unique.

At the same time, the credit union conducted its first member satisfaction survey, which revealed mediocre results. The combination of tremendous competition, low brand awareness, and marginally satisfied members pointed out, with great clarity, that the company's brand needed help.

Using the *Solving the Brand Puzzle* formula, MHV set out to discover the unique virtues of its particular brand, establish cornerstones to define the brand, and assimilate them into its corporate culture.

Getting started with Brand Discovery

MHV began Brand Discovery with the selection of a team comprised of representatives from every department and rank. I led the team which included front line and back office staff, management, supervisors, and executives. Over a period of one year, our branding team met regularly to tackle each phase of the discovery process.

Step 1: Recalling Heritage

As its first step toward shaping the future, the team began by looking into the past. What was commonly known among the present employees was that MHV was originally founded in the 1960's to support the financial needs of the employees of a large corporation which specialized in technology. Unfortunately, in the 90's, the manufacturing plant closed its doors. In spite of this setback, the credit union survived and continued to thrive by expanding its services to the community at large. This evolution was no simple matter, and involved strong leadership that overcame many challenges.

When the MHV team began probing Heritage, they realized that what was not commonly known were the details of MHV's unique history. From a historical perspective, the credit union had served the employees of a factory that helped the United States win the Cold War. Back then, the manufacturing plant produced a sophisticated target identification and acquisition radar for detecting the expected Soviet bomber attack on the United States. The system could even guide nuclear-tipped missiles to destroy those enemy aircraft. The system's processing memory, a paltry 64,000 bits, required a computer the size of a telephone booth. Today, that amount of processing power would be on a chip so small that it would be nearly invisible to the naked eye. The massive system contained 50,000 vacuum tubes (the predecessor of semiconductors) and required a fleet of tractor trailer trucks to transport it for installation!

When the branding team unearthed these surprising historic facts, they felt a huge sense of pride. They wondered how such an important piece of history had been forgotten. Remember our earlier example of how Irwin Bank had lost its connection to its Heritage and the story of Tobias Berkowitz? The same had occurred at MHV. Its rich Heritage had slowly faded. Only the recollection of some of the elder board members, when interviewed, shed any light on the company's history. Most of the credit union's 200+ current employees had little knowledge of the company's roots and character.

To ensure this rich Heritage would never be lost again, the branding team permanently captured it for future generations. They produced a video that included old public relations footage about the radar system, and current interviews with board members who recalled the era.

Step 2: Understanding the Purpose of Your Business

The Purpose of a Business is really a description of a company's ultimate benefit. For example, Volvo makes cars. But Volvo's reputation as a car manufacturer is based on building safe vehicles.

Therefore, in Volvo's case, exceptional safety is the ultimate benefit, adding value far beyond styling, comfort, and performance. Frankly, you could say that Volvo is fundamentally in the business of safety. This is similar to the other examples we talked about in chapter two, such as Starbucks being in the business of providing a neighborhood gathering experience, and Disney providing happiness.

The MHV team wanted to discover the ultimate benefit of the financial services it provided to its members. The following process helped them figure it out.

Exercise 2-A: Defining Member Loyalty

MHV had grown into a substantial player in its market area. To survive and prosper, the branding team realized that the company must embrace a more sophisticated attitude toward the member, one that would make the credit union more competitive on the playing field. The company needed to provide members with a better, more consistent member experience, and greater product value. It needed to differentiate itself.

Where to begin? The task seemed daunting. The one thing the team knew for certain was that the company needed to grow its base of loyal members. In order to better understand what creates member loyalty we turned to the Customer Loyalty Index tool, which was introduced to me in 2005 by Jack Salvetti from S.R. Snodgrass Company, a Pittsburgh, Pennsylvania consulting firm. The Customer Loyalty Index ranks loyalty based on two critical customer perceptions: those of Product Value and Customer Experience.

The first, Perception of Product Value, is based on the lowest price relative to the quality of the product. When a customer says, "I got a great deal," they perceive value. Customers may also perceive value when they receive free shipping for an online purchase, large portions at a restaurant, or great product "bundles" from a retail store.

The second, Quality of Customer Experience, includes how customers are treated. When surveyed customers have been pampered by employees, it's a pretty sure bet they will rate their experiences as excellent. Favorable customer experiences also come from the quality of the food, enjoyment of the atmosphere at a restaurant, an efficient online shopping experience, or any other rewarding interaction with a company.

Businesses that deliver the highest level of Perceived Product Value and/or Customer Experience achieve extreme customer loyalty. Those that deliver less achieve occasional, or worse still, only random customer loyalty, which is to say, not really loyalty at all, but a sort of apathy.

Using data from customer surveys, sales performance, and financial results, levels of loyalty can be charted on the Customer Loyalty Index. The degree of customer loyalty is determined by the position of the star along each axis of the chart.

In preparation for analyzing their own member loyalty, the MHV branding team analyzed customer loyalty in other companies. Based on their opinions, and available data, they mapped where they felt those companies should be on the Customer Loyalty Index.

Look where they placed Walmart on the Customer Loyalty Index chart. The position of the star shows how Walmart's strategic vision is polarized on selling low-priced, quality products, and not customer experience. This is not neces-

sarily a bad thing. Walmart is so good at it, that it can still build extreme loyalty, even attracting shoppers who don't necessarily "love" the experience of shopping there.

So you might be tempted to suggest that Walmart should work on improving its Customer Experience. Walmart's reason for not doing so would likely be that such changes would add too much cost with marginal return on the investment. Improving Walmart's Customer Experience would almost definitely require adding workers and training, resulting in price increases and potential loss of loyalty.

In the current age of automation, Walmart has achieved what Henry Ford did 100 years ago. Walmart invests heavily in automated processes to lower its cost of labor. Just as Ford did with his assembly line innovation in auto manufacturing, Walmart uses technology to manage its supply, logistics, and inventory chains. This requires a less-skilled work force which comes at a lower cost. Always the Low Price. Loyalty achieved.

In contrast to Walmart, the Customer Loyalty Index for Montano's Shoe Store, discussed in chapter two, clearly emphasizes service excellence. At Montano's, the importance placed on well-fitting shoes creates a strong Customer Experience. But since Montano's doesn't sell "cheap" shoes, prices are higher than you would see at a Target or Walmart. Although you may spend more, you get more for your money. It is the high quality of Customer Experience that enables Montano's to achieve Extreme Loyalty, even though The Perception of Value is average.

We have now seen how either Perception of Product Value or Quality of Customer Experience can result in Extreme Loyalty. Does anyone excel at both?

The American Customer Satisfaction Index[1], known

as ACSI, ranks companies based on a measure of both. Among the highest rated companies are some examples we have already talked about including Olive Garden, Red Lobster, and Southwest Airlines.

Southwest Airlines built its business as a low cost provider. But they also made a commitment to customer service.

Southwest's staff has fun with its passengers while providing a high level of courtesy. At the same time, it delivers value with low rates and few fees. So, Southwest achieves Extreme Loyalty by excelling at both Perception of Product Value and providing a high Quality of Customer Experience.

The branding team determined that the Customer Loyalty Index for MHV mirrored Montano's. Employees prided themselves on member service and the fact that the company had a unique, differentiating technology for retail banking delivery. It was the only financial institution in its area using live teller, video banking terminals. The technology provided members with 24/7 access to the credit union's tellers from every branch office location.

In addition, MHV was also the only financial institution using video banking with automobile drive-up convenience. It therefore was obvious that providing a strong member experience was an important part of the company's strategy.

As for Perception of Value, the branding team recognized that MHV was not the best interest rate provider in the market. Here's why: Instead of aggressively offering low rates to its members, which could adversely impact financial stability, the company focused on the preservation of its capital first. Therefore, its Perception of Value position on the Customer Loyalty Index ranked halfway up the axis.

When analyzing the Customer Loyalty Index, the team realized that no example was wholly right or wrong because no one company can be all things to all people. What was important was figuring out whether MHV should seek Extreme Loyalty based on Perception of Value, Member Experience, or a combination of both. This understanding set the stage for the next series of exercises.

Exercise 2-B: The Key Word exercise

The purpose of the Key Word exercise is to find common values of "what the company stands for." The branding team broke into four groups and independently listed key words they felt best described the company. These words related to expertise, character, or any other characteristic that defined the company.

Each group came up with fairly long lists. The value of the exercise really came into focus when a final, combined list isolated only the words that repeatedly appeared on the groups' multiple lists. A spirited discussion polarized around these words. And, although four separate lists had been created, the entire team easily agreed that the common words on the final list were the most significant.

Here are those words:

Technology – an attribute that is deeply rooted in the company history.

Community-minded – a consistent track record of community service and "local" pride.

Accessible/available – strong e-commerce and unique 24/7 teller access capability.

Trusted – high net worth, the key measure of financial soundness, is clearly a priority.

Member-focused – pride in delivering good member service.

What is interesting to note is that on all four lists, which produced close to 50 words, no one mentioned price. Obviously, price was not a priority. The team felt the company should be price-competitive, but not necessarily the price leader. A lesson learned in the exercise was that values are expressed not only by those key words that are listed, but by those that are absent as well.

Identifying these Key Words provided an initial reference point around which the team could begin to define a brand based on service and integrity.

Exercise 2-C: The Drilling-Down-to-the-Brand exercise

This exercise drills down to discover the real purpose of your business. Or, in other words, it helps you discover "what business you are *really* in." There are six steps in drilling down to your brand. The first three are about your company. The last three are about your customer.

MHV's branding team tackled this exercise as a whole group. With the result of their Key Word exercise taped on the wall, they debated, challenged, and ultimately answered the six questions that helped them discover MHV's "real" business. Here is how the exercise unfolded:

What is your line of business?
> Answer: Financial services.

...drilling down

What makes what you do special?
> Answer: We are convenient.

...drilling down

What makes you convenient?
> Answer: 24/7 live teller, e-commerce, office hours; good rates; loan application and underwriting procedures.

...drilling down

So what? What is the benefit?
> Answer: We make it easy for the member; we fit their schedules; we make banking flexible; we are sensitive to their needs.

...drilling down

How does the benefit make the member feel?
> Answer: Happy!

...drilling down

So what business are you <u>really</u> in?
> Answer: Improving lives, making dreams happen, providing peace of mind.

By drilling down, the team made the surprising discovery that the real business they were in was NOT financial services. Instead, the *real* business was actually in the benefit of those services to the member. They realized that financial services were a commodity. MHV's real purpose was to improve lives, make dreams happen, and to provide peace of mind. This was tested and validated by the answers to questions 2, 3, and 4.

Like Starbucks, which sells coffee but is *really* in the business of providing a gathering experience, and Disney, which sells entertainment but is *really* in the business of providing happiness, the MHV team had discovered the company's purpose: Improving the lives of its members.

Step 3: Establishing the Brand Cornerstones that define your Culture

In order to successfully deploy a Culture of brand consistency throughout the company, four critical Brand Cornerstones must first be established: Company Brand Standards, Staff Behavioral Guidelines, Customer Brand Statement, and Department Brand Integration. For this step, the MHV branding team turned to the world-class innovator of this process, the Walt Disney Company's Disney Institute.

Over time, MHV's Culture had evolved into one that lacked structure. Now, with over 200 employees working at 11 locations along a 60 mile path, its Culture had become inconsistent. It was the branding team's goal that, with the help of Disney Institute, they would design a structured Culture that would put the company on a path to delivering brand consistency.

Exercise 3-A: Establishing company Brand Standards

The MHV team moved forward to establish Company Brand Standards. They began by comparing the credit union's operations with Disney's four standards: Safety, Courtesy, Efficiency, and Show.

The team quickly agreed that Safety was critical. Their product, money, is so popular that people with guns try to steal it. Physical Safety had to be a priority. But, then a debate ensued about the importance of protecting the members' deposits. For a financial institution, Safety also implies the protection of member deposits. This debate helped to define the first Brand Standard: Safety and Soundness. Safety pertained to the physical well being of employees, and Soundness pertained to business practices.

Next, the team began to look at characteristics unique to financial institutions. What factors did financial institutions have to deal with that other companies, like Disney, did not? The answer was regulations and privacy.

Financial institutions have a long list of regulations that govern business practices. There are regulations pertaining to loans, deposits, and operating practices. They are all subject to an annual audit by federal regulators. These fall under what is known in the industry as "Compliance." Financial institutions are also governed by a long list of regulations designed to protect customer and member privacy and their personal information, known as "Confidentiality."

The branding team debated whether one of the two, Compliance or Confidentiality, was more important than the other and questioned, "Could they be combined?" Keeping in mind that Brand Standards are prioritized in order to function as a decision tree, the team decided to test the concept. Part of the team felt strongly that Confidentiality was more important. However, the other side quickly clarified priority by offering the example that a subpoena (representing Compliance) would trump any desire to keep information confidential. If information is demanded for legal purposes, it must be provided. Therefore, the MHV team established the first three standards as Safety and Soundness, Compliance, and Confidentiality.

Next, the team tackled service as a Company Brand Standard. It was with a sense of irony that the team realized they had already established the first three standards and hadn't even mentioned member service. Here they were, defining a brand built on lifestyle improvement, and yet member service, the topic the team originally felt would surely be listed first, had been subordinated by other priorities. This was a dramatic revelation.

The team concluded that the subject of member service should be segmented into two separate standards: Member Experience and Convenience. Member Experience was established as the service standard reflecting the "softer," human attributes that determine how service is presented and how it is perceived. Convenience was a separate standard that represented the "hard" elements of technology, and also brick and mortar facilities. Five standards had now been established and prioritized: Safety and Soundness, Compliance, Confidentiality, Member Experience, and Convenience.

One more Brand Standard was needed: Efficiency. Efficient operations conserve income by controlling expenses. That result ultimately delivers more value to the member in the form of better rates and lower fees.

The MHV branding team had successfully developed this effective list of Brand Standards:

1. Safety and Soundness
2. Compliance
3. Confidentiality
4. Member Experience
5. Convenience
6. Efficiency

These Brand Standards were consistent with the results of the earlier exercises which provided key words and defined what business the company was really in. They encompassed necessary operational and regulatory responsibility, and applied definition to member service. The Standards were tested as an employee decision tree and were determined to be easy to comprehend. The first critical Cornerstone of establishing Brand Standards was now a reality.

Presenting the brand consistently and appropriately

If you were to ask just about anyone to name a luxury car brand, they would most likely answer Lexus, Mercedes-Benz, or Cadillac. So imagine walking into a Mercedes-Benz dealership, and encountering a salesman in blue jeans, greeting you with "Hey, whassup?"

When considering the Culture associated with a luxury brand, wouldn't a well-groomed salesman in a suit, welcoming you with, "Thank you for choosing Mercedes-Benz. Let me introduce you to the world's finest automobiles," seem more appropriate?

This example demonstrates how something as minor as how your employees greet your members has a significant impact on how your brand is perceived. Now, expand this concept to every aspect of your business, and it becomes apparent why consistency and appropriateness are important.

Exercise 3-B: Creating a Customer Brand Statement

A Customer Brand Statement should encapsulate the results of previous Brand Discovery in one comprehensive message of commitment to the customer. In order to do so, the statement must satisfy these four objectives:

Define the customer.

State the company's character and philosophy.

State the purpose of what the company does.

State how the company's purpose is achieved.

To begin writing their own Brand Statement, the MHV team incorporated the above four objectives with the results of their Brand Discovery, which included key words, results of drilling down to the brand, and Brand Standards. They satisfied the four objectives in this way:

- **Define the customer** – For anyone who lives, works, worships, attends school or volunteers in [name of geographical market].
- **State the company's character and philosophy** – We are your trusted, financially sound, community credit union.
- **State the purpose of what the company does** – We make your life easier by providing personal and convenient financial solutions.
- **State how the company's purpose is achieved** – Our goal is to provide a member experience driven by innovative technology, reliable service, and easy access you can rely on.

This outline effectively and efficiently captured the results of Brand Discovery. The final Brand Statement that would ultimately be communicated to the member looked like this:

For anyone in need of financial services in Dutchess,
Orange, and Ulster Counties,
MHV is your trusted, financially sound,
community credit union.
We strive to make your life easier by providing
personal and convenient financial solutions.
Our goal is to provide an exceptional
member experience driven by
innovative technology, reliable service,
and easy access on which you can rely.

This Brand Statement was so well received that it was adopted as the company's mission statement by the Board of Directors. To have a Brand Statement so well developed that it could also communicate the mission was an outstanding accomplishment for the MHV Brand Discovery team.

Exercise 3-C: Developing Staff Behavioral Guidelines

The MHV team had defined its Brand Standards and understood that the next challenge was to establish appropriate brand consistency throughout the company. They needed to develop Staff Behavioral Guidelines and, once again, turned to Disney Institute. If MHV's 200 employees were to successfully provide a consistent member experience, why not learn from the company that had successfully done it with over 60,000 employees?

Disney has established seven simple guidelines to govern the way theme park employees treat their guests. The Walt Disney World Guest Service Guidelines[2] are:

1. **Make eye contact and smile!**
   Start and end every guest contact and communication with direct eye contact and a sincere smile.

2. **Greet and welcome each and every guest.**
   Extend the appropriate greeting to every guest with whom you come into contact. For example: "Good morning!"; "Welcome!"; "Have a good day!"; "May I help you?" Make guests feel welcome by providing a special differentiated greeting in each area.

3. Seek out guest contact.

It is the responsibility of every cast member to seek out guests who need help or assistance: Listen to guests' needs, answer questions, and offer assistance (For example: Taking family photographs).

4. Provide immediate service recovery.

It is the responsibility of all cast members to attempt, to the best of their abilities, to immediately resolve a guest service failure before it becomes a guest service problem. Always find the answer for the guest or find another cast member who can help the guest.

5. Display appropriate body language at all times.

It is the responsibility of every cast member to display approachable body language when on stage, including attentive appearance, good posture, and appropriate facial expression.

6. Preserve the "magical" guest experience.

Always focus on the positive, rather than the rules and regulations. Do not discuss personal or job-related problems in front of our guests.

7. Thank each and every guest.

Extend every guest a sincere thank-you at the conclusion of every transaction. Extend every guest a thank-you or similar expression of appreciation as he, or she, leaves your area.

The branding team initially thought some of the guidelines were too simple. Aren't these guidelines common sense? Make eye contact and smile? When they began considering certain staff members and the lineup of recent applicants, they realized that smiles did not exactly come naturally for a lot of people! In fact, for some, smiling isn't "cool." Soon the team was role playing, making eye contact while frowning and smiling while looking at the sky. Hmmm... maybe common sense needed to be taught after all.

Seek out guest contact? For some, walking up to a total stranger, looking them in the eye, smiling, and asking, "How can I help you?" was just too frightening an experience! Yet, how would you feel if you were next in line, and the teller just called out, "Next!"?

Sheepishly, members of the branding team admitted witnessing such behavior.

It was starting to make sense. Little things matter. Communicating expectations, even for the most basic of behaviors, was necessary. To justify the need, one only had to ask Chuck Urtin's poignant question: "What would *you* expect?"

The branding team kept it simple and logical, and settled on these five guidelines for staff behavior:

Smile, welcome, and thank every member.

Seek out member contact.

Be professional and courteous at all times.

Take ownership of service recovery.

Exceed expectations at every encounter.

Exercise 3-D: Department Brand Integration

Each department in the company plays a unique role in achieving the Brand Standards. The process by which all departments incorporate the Brand Standards into their daily functions is referred to as Brand Integration. The entire staff of each department works as a team to create a chart depicting how their department will achieve the Brand Standards. Every department activity is organized by the Brand Standards and further broken down by employee roles, available resources, and actions to be taken. *(See the Marketing Integration Grid at the end of this appendix)*

It was fascinating to observe how the marketing staff at MHV was drawn into the exercise. When they began to break down all of their activity, they became very spirited and proud. They had not considered the scope of their contribution to the company in such detail prior to engaging their integration assignment. As a result, the marketing staff developed a new appreciation for their role in the company, and how they impacted the company brand with their daily activities. Similar revelations also occurred in other departments.

Step 4: Write your book

Through the Brand Discovery process, each level of MHV now had an understanding of its role in solving its brand puzzle. They understood their Heritage. They had established a structure for presenting a consistent Brand Culture in the form of Standards, Guidelines, and Integration charts. And, they had defined the brand/mission statement for the member. The company brand was now understood, defined, and structured.

Finally, everything pertaining to the brand was published in a document, titled the *Brand Manual*, that served as the global brand reference for the entire company. This one comprehensive document became the brand "bible" for many aspects of the business including graphics consistency, management reference, and staff training.

Here are some examples of how the *Brand Manual* was put to use in the area of Sensory Experience. Before MHV began solving its brand puzzle, the company had been displaying six different sign versions at its branch office locations. Each sign used a modified version of the company logo. Today, all the signs have been brought into compliance with the graphics standards in the *Brand Manual*.

Prior to solving its brand puzzle, MHV's brand was never aligned with its strategy. Now, when creating strategic goals, management continually refers to the Brand Standards, published in the *Brand Manual*, for guidance.

Originally, the company training program was devoted to policy and operations. Now, a training class has been created to teach the Brand Cornerstones. The *Brand Manual* is used as a reference for maintaining cultural consistency now and into the future.

Summary

By discovering and integrating its brand, MHV continues to reap innumerable benefits. One inspiring example is the creation of a "Culture Team" that recognizes individual employees for exceptional acts of member service. Here's how it works: Managers submit nominations and a monthly winner is chosen by the Culture Team. Each winner receives $100 and is then eligible for an annual $2,500, best-of-the-best grand prize determined by the Culture Team. The program has dramatically improved both member service and employee morale. In fact, the contest has created an everyday spirit among employees, who seek to out-do one another, in their daily challenge of seeing who can provide the best service to members.

Marketing Integration Grid

Brand Standard	Employee Role
Safety & Soundness	Provide safe marketing materials Ensure event safety Ensure accuracy in communications Monitor and maintain budget Create and align campaigns that support business needs Protect company devices
Compliance	Ensure proper disclosures on all communications
Confidentiality	Secure customer information Maintain control of distribution of customer information Vendor due diligence
Customer Experience	Fresh content for marketing materials Plan customer events Support community Deliver compelling design and message Visual merchandising & branding Competitive awareness
Convenience	Workflow system Efficient distribution of marketing communications Efficient distribution of marketing/sales data Service Days (on site) Deliver 24/7 electronic access to CU information Ensure customer education
Efficiency	Effective internal communications Effective external communications Streamline marketing processes

Actions	Location & Resources
Inspect all material before distribution Develop planning team Follow proofing process Follow proofing process and budget procedures and review budget periodically Sales plan meetings, management communication Follow IT policies	Use trusted and known vendors Risk Management & Facilities Risk Management, Stakeholders Accounting, budget Market research, stakeholders, CFO Laptops, PCs, phones, cameras, dongles, disks, MIS
Compliance training and review process	Risk Management, stakeholders, compliance support, investment center marketing, regulations & policies
Use secure transmission resources Follow Risk Management policies and procedures Contracts and agreements in place with Risk Management review	sftp, https, encryption, password protection Marketing Analyst Risk Management
Review and update in conjunction with the marketing plan Coordination Coordination, target community events Create through collaborative brainstorming Provide direction, follow consistent design guide and planograms Analyze competition and make staff aware	Marketing Publicist, stakeholders (internal / external) Marketing meetings, conferences, branches, offsite venues Community Relations Committee; Senior Management Style guide, Marketing Publicist & Graphics Specialist, freelancers, consultants Consultants, planograms, experience zones, design guide, retail operations websites, ads, chambers, material
Communicate to staff and monitor daily Review at weekly meetings Analyze and share with stakeholders on a regular basis Contact CPs and schedule visits, deliver marketing materials Monitor, maintain and update Coordination	Marketing request procedures & intranet Intranet, website, Email, marketing channels Sales reports, branch analysis, customer survey, campaign tracking, ROI, google analytics, contact lists Corporate Partners & branches Website Seminars, financial literacy website content, topic experts, affiliates
Follow communications plan and execute in a timely fashion Follow communications plan and execute in a timely fashion Explore new resources	Intranet, email, branch sales visits, presentations, management, software Press releases, web, advertising, direct mail, call center, project management software Wire service, placement monitoring service, automated mail provider, web resources, programmers

 APPENDIX B

Culture Quiz
How does your culture rate?

Take the quiz and rate your organization's Culture. If you're not sure how to rank any one question, then it most likely rates a low score. Don't fool yourself. Be honest! As you proceed, subtotal each grade as a way to see where your organization may have strength or weakness. Remember, you are the only one who will see the result. This is just your assessment. You will likely be surprised by the result!

Rating Your Vision, Strategy & Leadership

SA = Strongly Agree
A = Agree
D = Disagree
SD = Strongly Disagree

THINKING LIKE A CUSTOMER-FOCUSED LEADER	SA	A	D	SD
My company believes that providing customers with a consistently differentiated experience will lead to profitable growth.	3	2	1	0
Our leaders at the top of the company are focused on the quality of our customers' experience.	3	2	1	0
Our leaders emphasize the importance of providing a consistent and differentiated customer experience.	3	2	1	0
Our leaders believe in the importance of having a customer experience strategy.	3	2	1	0
The interests of our customers are put ahead of the interests of internal departments.	3	2	1	0

Subtotal _____

ACTING LIKE A CUSTOMER-FOCUSED LEADER	SA	A	D	SD
Our company has established a clear vision statement that focuses on the customer.	3	2	1	0
In the eyes of our customers we have established a differentiated position from our competition in the marketplace.	3	2	1	0
Our leaders talk about our customers during key meetings.	3	2	1	0
Our leaders make it a point to visit with customers in person.	3	2	1	0
Our company's leaders follow through on our customer experience strategy.	3	2	1	0
There is clear accountability through all levels of staff for delivering an exceptional customer experience.	3	2	1	0

Subtotal _____

DEFINING CUSTOMER VALUES	SA	A	D	SD
We have identified the customers in our most valuable customer segments.	3	2	1	0
We have a real understanding of what our customers expect and value from us.	3	2	1	0
We have a real understanding of what our customers' functional needs and desires are.	3	2	1	0
We have identified which emotions the customer wants to feel while doing business with us.	3	2	1	0
We know which customer expectations impact loyalty (what makes them stay with us, expand their relationship with us, and recommend us).	3	2	1	0
We understand how customers perceive our performance vs. our competitors'.	3	2	1	0

Subtotal _____

DESIGNING & TESTING THE CUSTOMER EXPERIENCE	SA	A	D	SD
We understand what our customers' emotional needs are, and how to address them, so that customer service is perceived as exceptional.	3	2	1	0
We understand what elements are required to provide an exceptional customer experience.	3	2	1	0
We have a thorough understanding of whether or not we are providing an exceptional customer experience.	3	2	1	0
We understand which exceptional customer experiences are by design, and which are purely accidental.	3	2	1	0
Company leaders have defined and clearly communicated the Brand Cornerstones to employees and their important roles in delivering them.	3	2	1	0
Using customer feedback, we have designed new experiences which will deliver our Brand Standards in a way that is consistent and differentiated.	3	2	1	0
We consistently deliver experiences that align to our Brand Standards and therefore improve customer loyalty.	3	2	1	0

Subtotal _____

EQUIPPING AND INSPIRING EMPLOYEES	SA	A	D	SD
We have an internal communication plan to build understanding of, and commitment to, delivering an exceptional customer experience.	3	2	1	0
Leaders at all levels of our organization understand their roles as champions of our customers' experience and are prepared to lead its implementation.	3	2	1	0
Our leaders recognize and reward employees for meeting our customers' needs.	3	2	1	0
Our employees have a clearly defined role in delivering an exceptional customer experience.	3	2	1	0
Our employees are passionate about winning loyalty of our customers.	3	2	1	0
We have created a hiring profile based on attitude, skills, and knowledge, and we actively recruit new employees who fit this model.	3	2	1	0
Employees participate in ongoing training in order to understand our customer's needs and desires.	3	2	1	0
We have equipped our people with the skills and knowledge required to deliver an exceptional customer experience.	3	2	1	0
Employees at all levels understand how their daily actions are aligned to our customers' needs and desires.	3	2	1	0
Employees at all levels are empowered to use their judgment to make things right for the customer.	3	2	1	0

Subtotal _____

MEASURING AND REFINING PERFORMANCE	SA	A	D	SD
We have developed a comprehensive and fully integrated program to implement the customer experience strategy.	3	2	1	0
Business decisions are based on fulfilling the company's Brand Standards and are clearly communicated internally.	3	2	1	0
Customer data is used to manage the business.	3	2	1	0
Our internal processes are defined to enable us to provide an exceptional customer experience.	3	2	1	0
We have effective processes for internally evaluating and communicating the quality of our customers' experience.	3	2	1	0
Technology implementation is driven by the desire to improve our customers' experience, not solely for cost reductions or efficiency gains.	3	2	1	0
Our customers participate in product development.	3	2	1	0
Our back-office employees feel they are a part of the customer experience.	3	2	1	0

Subtotal _____

MEASURING CUSTOMER FEEDBACK	SA	A	D	SD
We have a formal process for collecting customer feedback regarding how well we are delivering the customer experience.	3	2	1	0
Customer feedback is continually gathered from all areas of customer contact.	3	2	1	0
Executives seek out customer feedback.	3	2	1	0
In addition to satisfaction, our survey system also measures customer loyalty and retention, and is used to identify needed operational changes.	3	2	1	0
Our organization always acts on feedback collected from customers.	3	2	1	0
Equal attention is paid to non-financial measures, such as customer satisfaction or loyalty, as to financial measures.	3	2	1	0
We know what our customers expect of our organization and also how well we are meeting those expectations.	3	2	1	0
Customer advocate leaders are in place among staff in all departments.	3	2	1	0

Subtotal _____

Tally up the subtotals in order to get your final score. How did your organization do? A perfect score is 150.

The first time I took the quiz, I was at a conference with approximately 100 other attendees. The highest score was in the 90's, and the room average was about 50. The score for Irwin Bank, where I worked at the time, was 48. We were told that of the 600 or so companies that had taken the quiz, the average was about 50. So if you got a low score, don't feel so bad. You are in broad company! Take a deep breath, and get started on changing your Culture!

Endnotes

INTRODUCTION   AN INTRODUCTION TO CUSTOMER SERVICE

1 Ostro, Stu, Senior Meteorologist. *Rough Night in Charleston and Savannah.* July 31, 2007. http:// www.weather.com/blog/weather/archive/200707.html (accessed June 5, 2011).
2 Yahoo! Finance. Yahoo! *Finance UK and Ireland.* http://uk.finance.yahoo.com/q/hp?s=DIS (accessed November 2012).

CHAPTER 1   THE POWER OF PROCESS

1 Pink, Daniel H. *A Whole New Mind: Why Right-Brainers Will Rule The Future.* 1st ed. New York: Riverhead Books, 2005.
2 Berk, Alan, interview by author. Son of Tobias Berkowitz. Greensburg, Pennsylvania, (2005).
3 In 1986, the Walt Disney Company established the Disney Institute to share its brand of business and leadership excellence with interested companies. www.disneyinstitute.com

CHAPTER 2   STRATEGIC VISION

1 Wal-Mart Stores, Inc. *Annual Report.* Bentonville, Arkansas: Wal-Mart Stores, 2009.
2 Walton, Sam, and John Huey. *Sam Walton: Made In America: My Story.* 1st. New York: Doubleday, 1992. Print. Similarly: http://www.walmart.com/cp/Always-Low-Prices/538350.
3 Terran, Ed. *Brief History of the Xerox Company.* November 30, 2008. http://www.articlesbase.com/ business-articles/brief-history-of-the-xerox-company-664924.html (accessed July 5, 2011).
4 Gartner DQ. *2006 U.S. Copier Market Share Monochrome and Color Copier.* February 2007. http://www.docstoc.com/docs/105393648/2006-US-Copier-Market-Share-Monochrome-and-Color-Copier- (accessed December 16, 2012).
5 Terran, 2008.
6 Edwards, Benj. *The computer mouse turns 40.* December 9, 2008. http://www.macworld.com/ article/1137400/mouse40.html (accessed December 2012).
7 Jobs, Steve, interview by Robert X. Cringely. Triumph of the Nerds: The Rise of Accidental Empires PBS. 1996.
8 Xerox Corp., A World Made Simpler...by Xerox. April 2012. http://www.youtube.com/ watch?v=kEnRQAz2Fqg (accessed August 2012).
9 Xerox Corp. Xerox at a Glance. 2012. http://www.xerox.com/ (accessed August 2012).
10 Yahoo! Finance. *Yahoo! Finance UK and Ireland.* http://uk.finance.yahoo.com/q/hp?s=XRX (accessed November 2012).
11 Yahoo! Finance. *Yahoo! Finance UK and Ireland.* http://uk.finance.yahoo.com/q/hp?s=IBM&a=07&b= 17&c=1981&d=07&e=17&f=2012&g=m&z=66&y=330 (accessed November 2012)

12 Farfan, Barbara. Starbucks *CEO Howard Schultz: Quotations About Building a World Class Brand.* May 08, 2012. http://retailindustry.about.com/od/frontlinemanagement/a/starbucksceohowardschulzquotes.htm (accessed December 16, 2012).

13 Kober, Jeff. *We Create Happiness.* October 25, 2007. http://www.mouseplanet.com/6976/We_Create_Happiness (accessed December 16, 2012).

14 Kinni, Theodore. (2001). *Be our guest: Perfecting the art of customer service.* Disney Editions. Print.

15 Investopedia. *Dictionary.* December 2012. http://www.investopedia.com/terms/s/swot.asp#axzz2DzGerfzT (accessed December 2012).

16 Flacy, Mike. *Dish Network shutting down a third of all remaining Blockbuster stores.* February 23, 2012. http://www.digitaltrends.com/home-theater/dish-network-shutting-down-a-third-of-all-remaining-blockbuster-stores/ (accessed June 5, 2012)./

17 Kary, Tiffany. *Blockbuster Wins Bankruptcy Court's Final Approval to Sell Assets to Dish.* April 26, 2011. http://www.bloomberg.com/news/2011-04-26/blockbuster-wins-final-bankruptcy-court-approval-to-sell-assets-to-dish.html (accessed July 10, 2012).

18 McTaggart, Jenny. *Wal-Mart vs. the world: still busily blanketing the U.S. with stores, the largest retailer is also becoming a major presence in countries around the globe. So far, its prospects are bigger than its problems.* Progressive Grocer, October 2003.

19 Galuszka, Peter. *Circuit City and the "Good to Great" Business Book Conundrum.* November 22, 2008. http://www.cbsnews.com/8301-505125_162-28241518/circuit-good-to-great-business-book-conundrum/ (accessed December 16, 2012).

20 Merced, Michael J. de la. *Circuit City to Liquidate After Sale Efforts Fail.* Edited by Andrew Ross Sorkin. January 16, 2009. http://dealbook.nytimes.com/2009/01/16/circuit city to liquidate after sale efforts fail (accessed December 15, 2012).

21 Sears Holdings Corporation. *Sears Holdings Reports Fourth Quarter and Full Year 2007 Results.* February 02, 2008. http://www.searsholdings.com/pubrel/pressOne.jsp?id=2008-02-28-0004764221 (accessed December 16, 2012).

CHAPTER 3   MANAGEMENT

1 Shapiro, Fred. *Quotes Uncovered: Running a Railroad and Famous Misquotes.* May 27, 2010. http://www.freakonomics.com/2010/05/27/quotes-uncovered-running-a-railroad-and-famous-misquotes/ (accessed December 16, 2012).

2 Guerra, Erick. *Valuing Rail Transit: Comparing Capital and Operating Costs to Consumer Benefits.* Working Paper, University of California, Berkeley Institute of Urban and Regional Development, 2010

3 Kaplan R S and Norton D P. "The Balanced Scorecard: measures that drive performance," *Harvard Business Review,* Jan. – Feb. 1992

4 Collins, Jim. *Good to Great.* New York, NY: Harper, 2001.

CHAPTER 4   CULTURE

1 "Our Company." *Darden.* Darden Concepts, Inc., 2011. Web. 06 Nov. 2011.

2 *Ibid.*

3 CNNMoney: A Service of CNN, Fortune & Money. "100 Best Companies To Work For: 2011." *CNNMoney.* Cable News Network. A Time Warner Company, 07 Feb. 2011. Web. 08, Nov. 2011.

4 Kaplan, Melanie D.G. *Red Lobster: Sustainability for the seafood lover of the future.* September 01, 2010. http://www.smartplanet.com/blog/pure-genius/red-lobster-sustainability-for-the-seafood-lover-of-the-future/4454?tag=search-river (accessed December 16, 2012).

5 Darden. "Sustainability at Darden." *http://www.darden.com.* 2010. http://www.darden.com/sustainability/downloads/2010-gri-full.pdf (accessed December 16, 2012)

6 Darden Concepts, Inc. Our Commitment to Quality. 2012. http://www.redlobster.com/our_
   quality_story/our_commitment_to_quality/ (accessed August 2012).
7 Southwest Airlines. *Fact Sheet*. December 16, 2012. http://www.southwest.com/html/about-
   southwest/history/fact-sheet.html#fleet (accessed December 16, 2012).
8 Southwest Airlines. *Our Culture*. December 16, 2012. http://www.southwest.com/html/about-
   southwest/careers/culture.html (accessed December 16, 2012).
9 Lang, Julie B. and Govindarajan, Vijay. "Southwest Airlines Corporation." William F. Achtmeyer
   Center for Global Leadership, Tuck School of Business at Dartmouth, 2002.
10 Southwest Airlines. *Fact Sheet*. December 16, 2012. http://www.southwest.com/html/about-
   southwest/history/fact-sheet.html#fleet (accessed December 16, 2012).
11 Anderson, Eric. "Albany Had Highest Airfare in State DOT Finds." *timesunion.com*. Hearst
   Communications, 02 Aug. 2010. Web. 08 Nov. 2011.
12 American Customer Satisfaction Index. *Benchmarks By Industry*. 2012. http://www.theacsi.
   org/?option=com_content&view=article&id=147&catid=14&Itemid=212&i=Airlines (accessed
   December 16, 2012).

CHAPTER 5   SENSORY EXPERIENCE

1 American Customer Satisfaction Index. *ACSI Scores: National, Sector & Industry*. December 2012.
   http://www.theacsi.org/about-acsi/acsi-benchmarks-national-sector-industry (accessed December
   17, 2012).
2 Safer, M. (Performer) (2011). The flavorists: Tweaking Tastes and Creating Cravings [Television
   series episode]. In Streeter, R. (Executive Producer), *60 Minutes*. New York: CBS. Retrieved
   from http://www.cbsnews.com/8301-18560_162-57330816/the-flavorists-tweaking-tastes-and-
   creating-cravings/
3 Interbrand. *Best Global Brands 2012*. http://www.interbrand.com/en/best-global-brands/2012/
   Best-Global-Brands-2012 (accessed November 15, 2012).
4 Interbrand. *Best Retail Brands 2012*. http://www.interbrand.com/en/BestRetailBrands/2012-Best-
   Retail-Brands.aspx (accessed November 15, 2012).
5 Weston, J. (2009, May 11). http://www.australiantrademarkslawblog.com/2009/05/articles/
   miscellaneous-intellectual-pro/annual-nicholas-weston-tattooed-brands-global-survey-2009-
   results (accessed January 10, 2011)

CHAPTER 6   THE DIGITAL BRAND

1 Roggio, Armando. *Ecommerce Know-How: Amazon Can Sell Your Products and Advertise Them,
   Too*. February 26, 2009. http://www.practicalecommerce.com/articles/986-Ecommerce-Know-
   How-Amazon-Can-Sell-Your-Products-and-Advertise-Them-Too (accessed December 17, 2012).
2 Trachtenberg, Joseph Checkler and Jeffrey A. "Bookseller Borders Begins a New Chapter...11."
   The Wall Street Journal, February 17, 2011.
3 Yahoo! Finance. *Yahoo! Finance UK and Ireland*. http://uk.finance.yahoo.com/q/hp?s=AMZN
   (accessed December 2012).
4 Marshall, Ken. *Move to online causes decline of travel agency jobs*. October 14, 2009. http://www.
   cleveland.com/pdgraphics/index.ssf/2009/10/move_to_online_causes_decline.html (accessed December
   17, 2012).
5 Kitten, Tracy. "Global Breach Date Now Jan. 2011." *CU Info Security*, May 16, 2012.
6 Poulson, Kevin. *Kingpin*. New York: Random House, 2011.
7 Chen, Tim. "Identity Theft: Your Chances of Being a Victim." *US News and World Report Money*,
   March 23, 2011.
8 Sony, Corp. *Sony Corp. Info - News Releases*. May 15, 2011. http://www.sony.net/SonyInfo/News/
   Press/201105/11-0515E/index.html (accessed November 17, 2012).
9 Sutter, John D. *Gamers fuming over PlayStation hack*. April 28, 2011. http://www.cnn.com/2011/
   TECH/gaming.gadgets/04/27/sony.playstation.hack.reaction/index.html (accessed December 17,
   2012).

CHAPTER 7   BE A BRAND CRITIC

1 Clifford, Catherine. A *bitter brew for Starbucks*. November 10, 2008. http://money.cnn.
   com/2008/11/10/news/companies/starbucks_earnings/index.htm (accessed December 18, 2012).
2 Miller, Claire Cain. *A Changed Starbucks. A Changed C.E.O.* March 12, 2011. http://www.
   nytimes.com/2011/03/13/business/13coffee.html?_r=0 (accessed December 18, 2012).
3 Yahoo! Finance. *Yahoo! Finance UK and Ireland.* http://uk.finance.yahoo.com/q/hp?s=SBUX
   (accessed November 2012).

APPENDIX A   BRAND DISCOVERY CASE STUDY

1 The American Consumer Satisfaction Index, or ACSI, reports scores on a 0-100 scale at the
   national level and produces indexes for 10 economic sectors, 47 industries, more than 225
   companies, and over 200 federal or local government services. In addition to the company-level
   satisfaction scores, ACSI produces scores for the causes and consequences of customer satisfaction
   and their relationships. The measured companies, industries, and their sectors are broadly
   representative of the U.S. economy serving American households.
2 Kinni, Theodore. (2001). *Be our guest: Perfecting the art of customer service*. Disney Editions. Print.

Index

ABOUT ROBERT MICHAUD

Robert Michaud has worked in the sales, marketing, advertising, and customer service industries for over 35 years. During this time, he developed award-winning campaigns and projects for several national and regional clients, in a wide range of businesses including retail, manufacturing, home improvement, and banking. Robert is currently the Chief Marketing Officer for a financial institution in New York.